I0448401

September 2013

CARGO TANK TRUCKS

Improved Incident Data and Regulatory Analysis Would Better Inform Decisions about Safety Risks

GAO-13-721

CARGO TANK TRUCKS

Improved Incident Data and Regulatory Analysis Would Better Inform Decisions about Safety Risks

GAO Highlights

Highlights of GAO-13-721, a report to congressional committees

Why GAO Did This Study

Cargo tank trucks deliver gasoline and other flammable liquids daily for consumer use. Trucks are loaded and unloaded through external bottom lines that, after loading, may contain up to 50 gallons of liquid and are known as "wetlines." Concerns have been raised about the safety of wetlines, since a collision may rupture them, releasing flammable liquid and possibly causing fatalities and property damage. PHMSA is responsible for regulating the safe transportation of hazardous materials and has proposed rules prohibiting the transport of flammable liquids in wetlines.

In 2012, The Moving Ahead for Progress in the 21st Century Act required GAO to examine this issue. This report discusses (1) the extent that PHMSA's data reliably identify wetline safety risks, (2) options for addressing wetline safety risks, and (3) how well PHMSA has assessed the costs and benefits of addressing these risks through regulation. GAO analyzed PHMSA's wetline incident data for 1999 to 2011, reviewed PHMSA's regulatory cost-benefit analyses, and interviewed agency officials and industry and safety stakeholders.

What GAO Recommends

DOT should improve its wetline incident data by requiring carriers to specifically report wetline incidents and by improving its information on incident consequences. DOT should also address uncertainty in the assumptions and data underlying its regulatory cost-benefit analysis. DOT did not agree or disagree with the recommendations, but provided technical comments.

View GAO-13-721. For more information, contact Susan A. Fleming at (202) 512-2834 or flemings@gao.gov.

What GAO Found

The Department of Transportation's (DOT) Pipeline and Hazardous Materials Safety Administration's (PHMSA) incident data cannot be used to reliably identify risks from incidents involving collisions with and spills from tank trucks' bottom lines ("wetlines") because the incidents are not specifically identified in PHMSA's database and the data contain inaccuracies. PHMSA requires carriers to report hazardous material incidents, but the reporting form does not specifically capture wetline incidents. PHMSA officials identify wetline incidents through a resource-intensive process of reviewing carrier-reported incident narratives and other information. However, GAO found that the narratives do not always clearly indicate whether an incident is wetline related and that information about the consequences of incidents, including fatalities, is not always accurate. PHMSA has made efforts to improve its data, such as adding quality checks, but this has not affected how wetline incidents are reported, and inaccuracies remain.

One technology to purge liquid from wetlines exists, but use of this system is limited, and industry and safety stakeholders expressed concerns about it, such as concerns about the safety of retrofitting existing trucks with the device and its cost. Although other options have been proposed to address wetline risks, none has been pursued, and there are concerns about their safety and feasibility as well. For example, wetlines could be drained at loading terminals, but this creates issues over storing the drained fuel and whether it could be resold.

PHMSA analyzed the costs and benefits of its proposed 2011 rule to prohibit transportation of flammable liquids in unprotected wetlines, but did not account for uncertainties in its analytical assumptions and limitations in the underlying incident data. For example, PHMSA's analysis overstated the number of fatalities the proposed rule would prevent when considering actual past incidents. Furthermore, PHMSA based its cost analysis on the assumption that carriers would install a certain type of wetline purging system, but its limited adoption makes that cost uncertain. Federal guidance recommends that agencies account for uncertainty in regulatory analysis, such as limitations in PHMSA's data and uncertainty in its assumptions. Without having done so, PHMSA's analysis may not accurately represent the costs and benefits of its proposed rule.

Examples of Wetline Incidents

Minor incident scenario	Severe incident scenario
Truck hits barrier pole at gas station. One of the wetlines is damaged resulting in a small spill.	A passenger vehicle goes through a stop sign and underruns a tank truck. One or more of the truck's wetlines are sheared off, resulting in a larger gasoline spill and a fire.

Source: GAO.

_____ United States Government Accountability Office

Contents

Figures

Abbreviations

DOT	Department of Transportation
hazmat	hazardous material
MAP-21	Moving Ahead for Progress in the 21st Century Act
NTSB	National Transportation Safety Board
OMB	Office of Management and Budget
PHMSA	Pipeline and Hazardous Materials Safety Administration

September 11, 2013

The Honorable John D. Rockefeller, IV
Chairman
The Honorable John Thune
Ranking Member
Committee on Commerce, Science, and Transportation
United States Senate

The Honorable Bill Shuster
Chairman
The Honorable Nick J. Rahall, II
Ranking Member
Committee on Transportation and Infrastructure
House of Representatives

Americans rely on flammable liquids such as gasoline for daily personal and industrial use, but transporting these liquids poses inherent safety risks to people and property. Cargo tank trucks transporting flammable liquids in the United States are loaded and unloaded through external pipes under the tank compartments. These pipes, when they contain flammable liquid, are known as "wetlines" and can collectively carry up to 50 gallons of liquid per truck. The National Transportation Safety Board (NTSB), among others, has identified wetlines as a potential hazard because a broadside collision with a tank truck can rupture the wetlines, spilling flammable liquid and creating the potential to fuel fires and therefore increased damage and fatalities from such incidents. In 1997, such an incident occurred in Yonkers, New York, when a passenger car collided with a tank truck under a highway overpass. The collision ruptured the truck's wetlines, resulting in a passenger fatality and the destruction of the overpass. The incident, cleanup, and subsequent infrastructure repairs created significant and costly traffic delays in the region.

In 1998, after investigating the Yonkers incident, NTSB recommended that the Department of Transportation (DOT) prohibit transportation of all hazardous materials in wetlines. DOT subsequently proposed rules to prohibit the transportation of flammable liquids in unprotected external product piping ("wetlines"), but did not adopt final rules in those proceedings. In January 2011, the Pipeline and Hazardous Materials Safety Administration (PHMSA), an operating administration of DOT, again proposed a rule to prohibit the transportation of flammable liquids in unprotected wetlines and released an initial analysis of the proposed rule's costs and benefits. PHMSA updated its cost-benefit analysis in March 2012, but did not release this version publicly. The Moving Ahead for Progress in the 21st Century Act (MAP-21), enacted in July 2012, temporarily stopped PHMSA from issuing a final wetlines rule except in very specific circumstances[1] and required us to examine the risks of and alternatives to transporting flammable liquids in wetlines. In this report we discuss: (1) the extent that PHMSA's data can be used to reliably identify wetline safety risks, (2) options for addressing wetline safety risks, and (3) how well PHMSA has assessed the costs and benefits of addressing these risks through regulation.

To evaluate the extent that PHMSA's data can be used to reliably identify wetline safety risks, we examined PHMSA's process for identifying wetline incidents among its reported hazardous materials (hazmat) incidents, analyzed how useful PHMSA's incident data from January 1999 through March 2011 are for identifying such incidents,[2] and examined whether these data accurately captured information about the incidents' consequences. We reviewed the reliability of these data by examining them for missing data and inconsistencies, reviewing PHMSA's process for obtaining wetline incident data and maintaining them in the agency's incident database, and reviewing the agency's related internal controls. We concluded that the data were sufficiently reliable for the purposes of our report. To describe options for addressing wetline safety risks, we identified options by reviewing documents filed in the current and prior PHMSA wetline safety rulemakings and interviewing petroleum and related transportation industry and safety stakeholders (see app. I for a list of stakeholders we interviewed). We also asked stakeholders about their views on the advantages and disadvantages of these options and reviewed comments filed in the most recent PHMSA wetline rulemaking. We placed particular focus on examining the wetline purging system, because it is the option used in PHMSA's wetlines rulemaking analysis and the only option we identified that has been installed to address wetline risks. To evaluate how well PHMSA has assessed the costs and benefits of its January 2011 proposed wetline rule, we reviewed PHMSA's

---

[1]Pub L. No. 112-141, 126 Stat. 405, 840-41 (2012). Section 33015 of MAP-21 prohibits DOT from issuing a wetlines final rule prior to either the completion of our mandated study or until July 2014, whichever is earlier, unless DOT determines that a risk to public safety, property, or the environment is present or an imminent hazard exists and that the regulations will address the risk or hazard.

[2]We examined incident data from January 1999 through March 2011 because this is the period of time of the incidents PHMSA used to support its wetline rulemaking.

associated regulatory cost-benefit analysis, examined the reliability of PHMSA's supporting wetline incident data used to inform the analysis, and interviewed PHMSA officials about their efforts. See appendix I for a more detailed description of our objectives, scope and methodology.

We conducted this performance audit from September 2012 to September 2013 in accordance with generally accepted government auditing standards. Those standards require that we plan and perform the audit to obtain sufficient, appropriate evidence to provide a reasonable basis for our findings and conclusions based on our audit objectives. We believe that the evidence obtained provides a reasonable basis for our findings and conclusions based on our audit objectives.

Background

Flammable Liquid Distribution

Every day, tens of thousands of cargo tank trucks transport hazardous materials classified as flammable liquids (primarily gasoline and fuel oil) for sale in the United States.[3] This involves some safety risk because of the volatile nature of flammable liquids, the volume of liquid transported (up to 9,200 gallons per truck), and the numbers of trucks and passenger vehicles on the road. Tank trucks that carry flammable liquids have three main components—the truck, the trailer, and the cargo tank. The tank may be divided into several compartments—usually four or five—allowing the truck to carry different petroleum products in a single trip, such as different grades of gasoline and diesel fuel. Although the design of cargo tank trucks can vary depending on the model and manufacturer, the components in figure 1 are common features.

---

[3]The exact number of cargo tank trucks operating in the United States is unknown since DOT does not track this information. For the purposes of the proposed wetline rule, PHMSA's regulatory assessment assumes a total of 27,000 tank trucks would be affected by a rule. Citing others' research, NTSB has indicated that other estimates have ranged from about 10,000 to 60,000 tank trucks. See NTSB, *Safety Recommendation, H-11-1* (Washington, D.C.: Sept. 2, 2011).

Figure 1: Cargo Tank Truck Components That Pertain to Loading, Transporting, and Unloading of Flammable Liquids

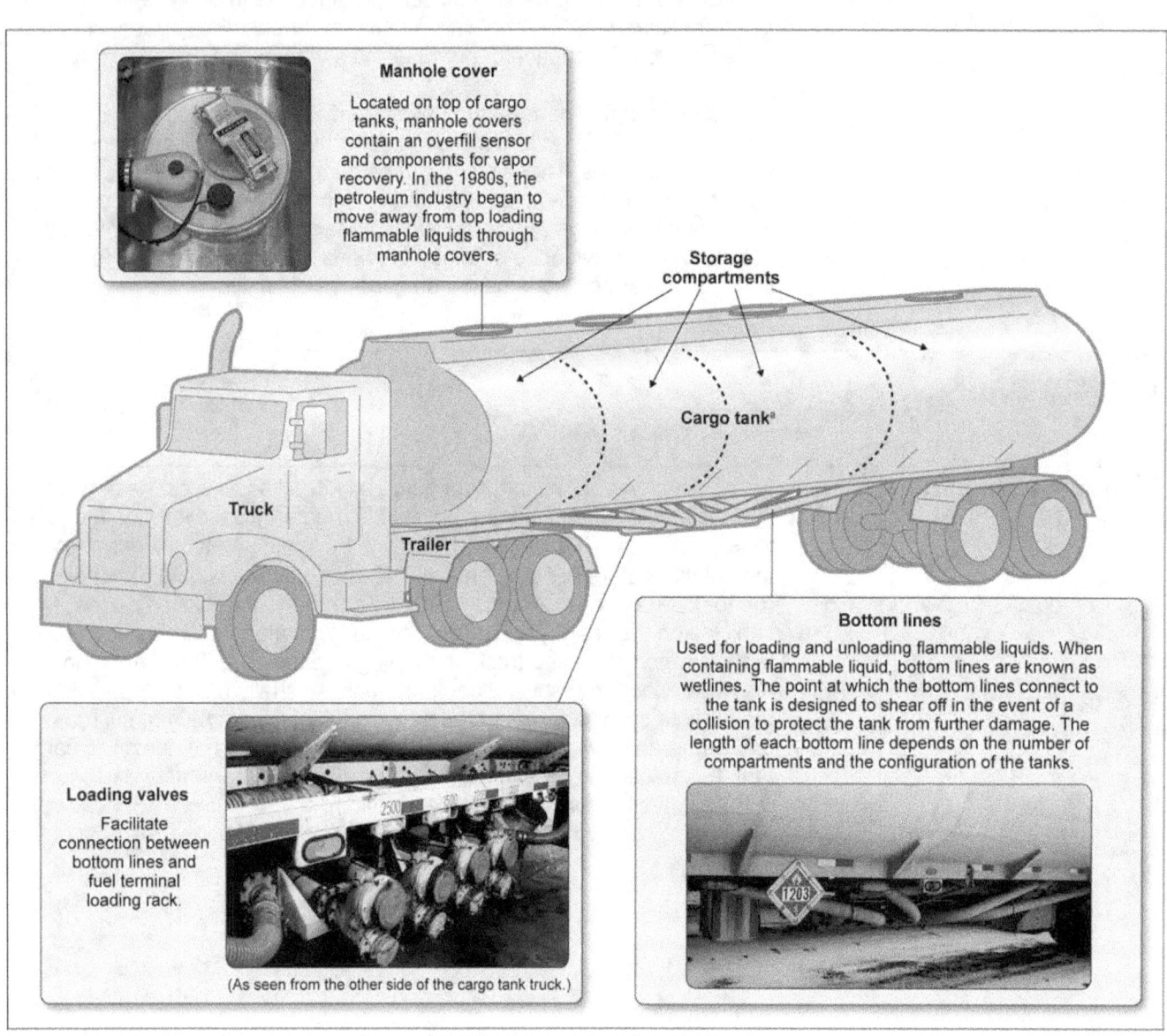

Manhole cover

Located on top of cargo tanks, manhole covers contain an overfill sensor and components for vapor recovery. In the 1980s, the petroleum industry began to move away from top loading flammable liquids through manhole covers.

Storage compartments

Cargo tank[a]

Truck

Trailer

Bottom lines

Used for loading and unloading flammable liquids. When containing flammable liquid, bottom lines are known as wetlines. The point at which the bottom lines connect to the tank is designed to shear off in the event of a collision to protect the tank from further damage. The length of each bottom line depends on the number of compartments and the configuration of the tanks.

Loading valves

Facilitate connection between bottom lines and fuel terminal loading rack.

(As seen from the other side of the cargo tank truck.)

Source: GAO and photos from National Tank Truck Carriers.

[a]Weight restrictions limit a cargo tank truck's operating capacity to between 7,500 and 9,200 gallons of liquid, which is usually less than the tank's total capacity.

The rule proposed by PHMSA in January 2011 would require that flammable liquids be eliminated from bottom loading and unloading lines, such as by purging the bottom lines of product, or that bottom lines be protected with approved bottom protection devices.[4] The rule would apply to cargo tank trucks that typically transport gasoline, diesel, and fuel oil from distribution terminals—of which there are nearly 400 nationwide—to retail outlets or gas stations (see fig. 2).

---

[4]Bottom damage protection devices must meet the requirements of 49 C.F.R. §178.337-10, 49 C.F.R. §178.345-8(b), or the accident damage protection requirements of the specification under which the cargo tank motor vehicle was manufactured.

Figure 2: A Typical Process for Loading, Transporting, and Unloading Cargo Tank Trucks Carrying Flammable Liquids

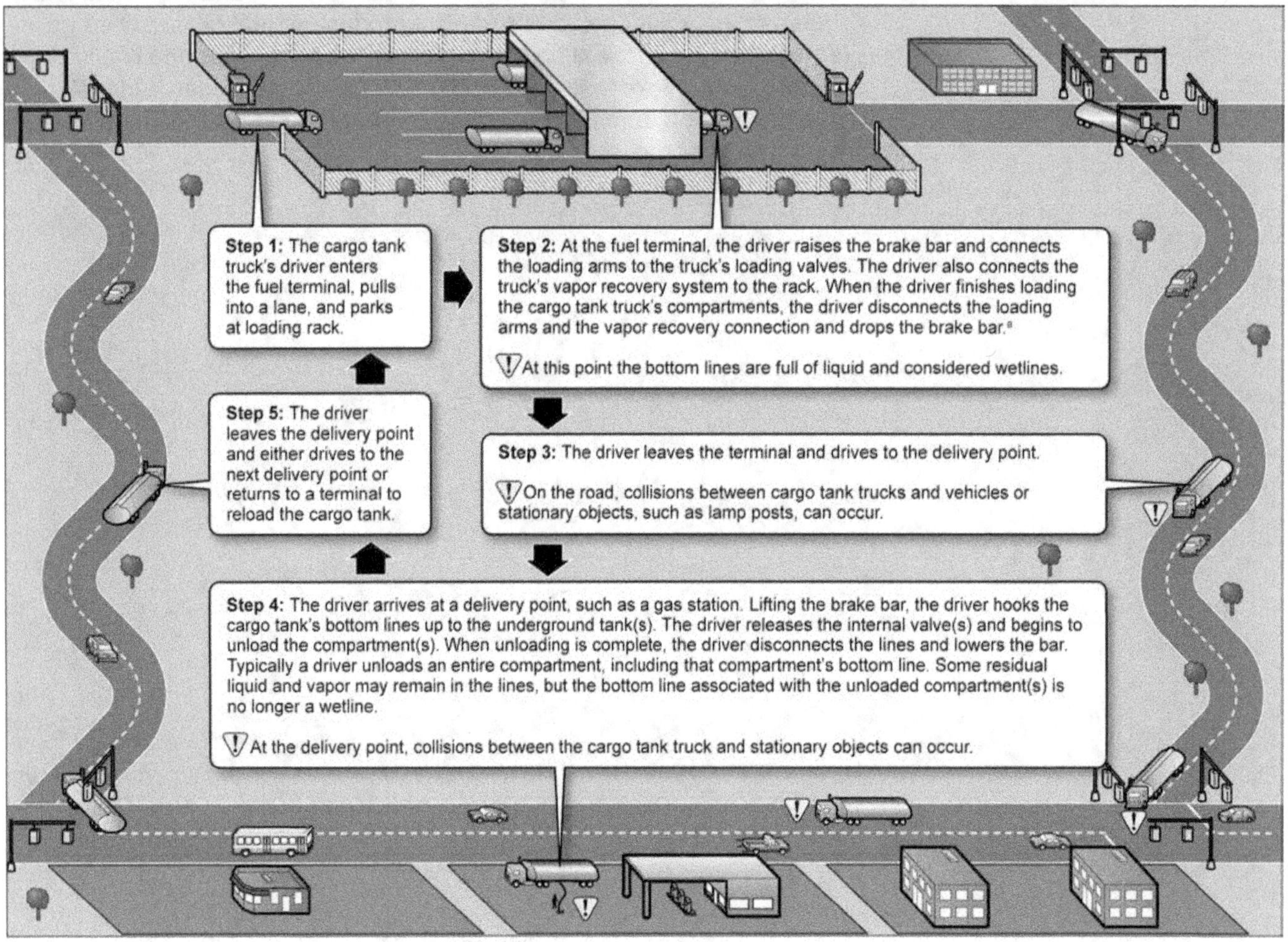

Step 1: The cargo tank truck's driver enters the fuel terminal, pulls into a lane, and parks at loading rack.

Step 2: At the fuel terminal, the driver raises the brake bar and connects the loading arms to the truck's loading valves. The driver also connects the truck's vapor recovery system to the rack. When the driver finishes loading the cargo tank truck's compartments, the driver disconnects the loading arms and the vapor recovery connection and drops the brake bar.[a]

⚠ At this point the bottom lines are full of liquid and considered wetlines.

Step 5: The driver leaves the delivery point and either drives to the next delivery point or returns to a terminal to reload the cargo tank.

Step 3: The driver leaves the terminal and drives to the delivery point.

⚠ On the road, collisions between cargo tank trucks and vehicles or stationary objects, such as lamp posts, can occur.

Step 4: The driver arrives at a delivery point, such as a gas station. Lifting the brake bar, the driver hooks the cargo tank's bottom lines up to the underground tank(s). The driver releases the internal valve(s) and begins to unload the compartment(s). When unloading is complete, the driver disconnects the lines and lowers the bar. Typically a driver unloads an entire compartment, including that compartment's bottom line. Some residual liquid and vapor may remain in the lines, but the bottom line associated with the unloaded compartment(s) is no longer a wetline.

⚠ At the delivery point, collisions between the cargo tank truck and stationary objects can occur.

Source: GAO.

[a]The brake bar interlock is a system that, when activated, applies the truck's parking brakes. A driver lifts the brake bar to access the truck's loading valves, immobilizing the truck during loading or unloading.

In the 1980s, to address volatile organic compound emission reduction requirements,[5] as well as worker safety issues, the petroleum industry changed cargo tank-loading procedures from loading through the manhole covers on the top of the truck to loading through the bottom lines. Prior to this change, the bottom lines were used for unloading only and therefore generally did not contain more than a residual amount of flammable liquids during transport. In using bottom lines for loading, because the lines are at the lowest point on the truck, they do not drain into the main tanks but contain fuel. Bottom lines containing fuel are referred to as "wetlines."

Wetline Incidents and Reporting

Wetline incidents result from collisions involving tank trucks that lead to the release of flammable liquid from wetlines. Such incidents range from easily contained spills to catastrophic situations. Carriers that transport hazardous materials, including flammable liquids like gasoline, are required to report incidents involving the release of hazmat to PHMSA.[6] Carriers, for example, must submit an electronic or paper incident reporting form within 30 days of the incident. This form is designed to provide information about the vehicle and container involved in the incident, the component of the container that failed, the type and quantity of product released, and, if applicable, fatalities, injuries, and the dollar value of significant damages associated with the incidents.[7] The form also includes a space for carriers to write a descriptive narrative of the incident. Information from these forms appears in PHMSA's publicly

---

[5]Volatile organic compounds present in vented gas are contributors to elevated ozone and haze.

[6]The carrier is the company with physical control of the shipment during its transportation, which may or may not be the same as the shipper, i.e., the company originally providing the product. Carriers transporting flammable liquids may be oil companies or tank truck carriers that haul a variety of products.

[7]In most cases, an accidental release of hazmat from a cargo tank will require a written report within 30 days of the incident, specifically, a Hazardous Material Incident Report, Form DOT F 5800.1. This report is also required for damage to the lading system, even without a release of hazardous materials. Additionally, immediate reporting may be required to the National Response Center, a Coast Guard-operated sole national point-of-contact for all oil and chemical discharges into the environment in the United States. See 49 C.F.R. §171.15-16. Although PHMSA's incident-reporting regulations exempt certain specified small releases, such as from the connection or disconnection of loading or unloading lines, the PHMSA regulations require the reporting of any unintentional release of a hazardous material, such as gasoline, and do not otherwise exempt releases below a specified minimum quantity.

available web-based incident database.[8] According to PHMSA, it uses the database for its safety oversight work, including regulatory efforts.

While most wetline incidents identified by PHMSA did not result in fires, spilled flammable liquid can ignite and create the potential for fatalities as well as increased property and environmental damages. Incidents may be the result of a tank truck striking a stationary object or a moving passenger vehicle striking the tank truck. Figure 3 shows examples of two types of wetline incidents.

---

[8]PHMSA's incident database is available at https://hazmatonline.phmsa.dot.gov/IncidentReportsSearch/ (accessed May 14, 2013).

Figure 3: Examples of Wetline Incidents

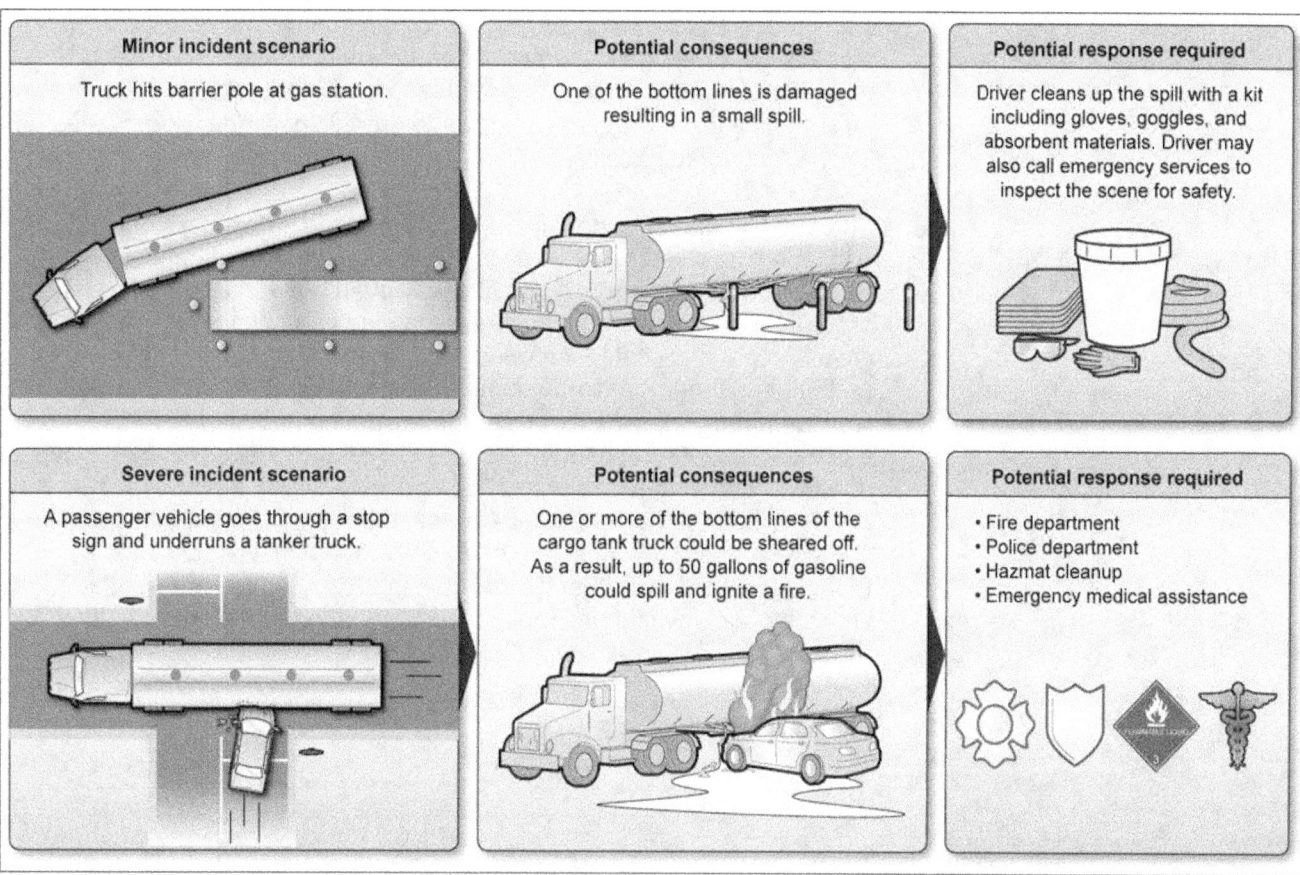

Source: GAO.

DOT Wetline Initiatives, 1989–2012

PHMSA is responsible for regulating the safe and secure transportation of hazardous materials to reduce the risks to people and the environment. In 1989 and 1990, PHMSA's predecessor, the Research and Special Programs Administration, promulgated final rules that prohibited external product piping, such as bottom lines, from retaining hazardous liquids unless the cargo tank truck is equipped with bottom damage protection devices.[9] Citing concerns about the potential costs of modifying fuel

---

[9]See, e.g., 54 Fed. Reg. 24982 (June 12, 1989); 55 Fed. Reg. 21035 (May 22, 1990); 55 Fed. Reg. 37028 (Sep. 7, 1990).

GAO-13-721 Cargo Tank Trucks

terminal operations, the lack of data on incidents, and the lack of information on possible alternatives to empty wetlines after bottom loading, the Research and Special Programs Administration exempted tanks transporting gasoline and other flammable liquids from the regulation.[10] Thus, the resulting regulations, in general, pertain to certain poisonous liquids, oxidizer liquid, liquid organic peroxide, or corrosive liquids, but not to gasoline.[11]

The 1997 Yonkers incident drew attention to the safety risks of wetlines because it involved a fatality as well as unusually high damages. Specifically, its destruction of a highway overpass resulted in severe property damage, and the incident's location in a congested area led to severe economic costs. Following NTSB's recommendation that DOT prohibit transport of hazardous materials in wetlines,[12] DOT (through the Research and Special Programs Administration and later PHMSA) submitted a draft proposed rule to the Office of Management and Budget (OMB) to address the issue in 2000 and later issued a proposed rule in 2004. PHMSA withdrew its 2004 proposed rulemaking in 2006 because it concluded that the benefits of the rule would not justify the costs.[13] PHMSA proposed another wetline rule in 2011. Figure 4 shows the timeline of key events and major regulatory efforts to address wetline risks.

---

[10]A key concern over addressing this issue at the terminal, which industry stakeholders reiterated to us, is that fuel taxes are assessed through a metering system once the product is loaded onto a truck. To then drain some of the product from the wetlines would create an accounting problem, in addition to the issue of whether the product could be resold or would have to be disposed of.

[11]49 C.F.R. § 173.33(e).

[12]The NTSB considers the practice of transporting flammable liquids in wetlines to be an unsafe practice and contends that incidents similar to the Yonkers incident are likely to occur in the future. 76 Fed. Reg. 4847, 4848 (Jan. 27, 2011).

[13]Office of Management and Budget, *Regulatory Analysis,* OMB Circular No. A-4 (Sept. 17, 2003), which implements Executive Order 12866, *Regulatory Planning and Review* (Washington, D.C.: Sept. 30, 1993), requires agencies to assess the costs and benefits of specified types of proposed significant regulatory actions to analyze whether the expected benefits of the regulation are likely to justify its costs.

Figure 4: Timeline of Key Events and Federal Regulatory Actions on Wetlines

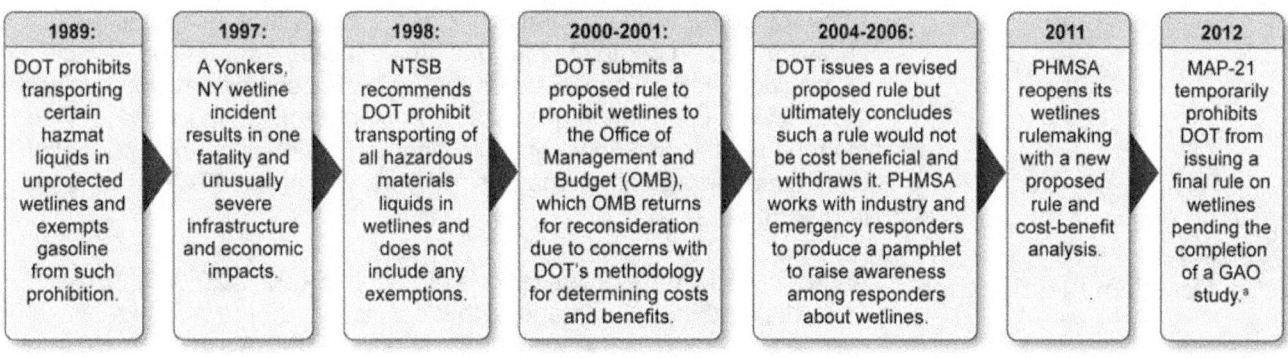

1989:	1997:	1998:	2000-2001:	2004-2006:	2011	2012
DOT prohibits transporting certain hazmat liquids in unprotected wetlines and exempts gasoline from such prohibition.	A Yonkers, NY wetline incident results in one fatality and unusually severe infrastructure and economic impacts.	NTSB recommends DOT prohibit transporting of all hazardous materials liquids in wetlines and does not include any exemptions.	DOT submits a proposed rule to prohibit wetlines to the Office of Management and Budget (OMB), which OMB returns for reconsideration due to concerns with DOT's methodology for determining costs and benefits.	DOT issues a revised proposed rule but ultimately concludes such a rule would not be cost beneficial and withdraws it. PHMSA works with industry and emergency responders to produce a pamphlet to raise awareness among responders about wetlines.	PHMSA reopens its wetlines rulemaking with a new proposed rule and cost-benefit analysis.	MAP-21 temporarily prohibits DOT from issuing a final rule on wetlines pending the completion of a GAO study.[a]

Source: GAO.

[a]Section 33015 of MAP-21 prohibits DOT from issuing a wetlines final rule prior to either the completion of GAO's mandated study or until July 2014, whichever is earlier, unless DOT determines that a risk to public safety, property, or the environment is present or an imminent hazard exists and that the regulations will address the risk or hazard.

PHMSA's Incident Data Cannot Be Used to Reliably Identify Wetline Incidents, Although Efforts to Improve Data Quality Have Been Implemented

PHMSA's incident data do not reliably capture the risks and consequences of wetline incidents because these incidents are not specifically identified in its database, and PHMSA's incident data also contain inaccuracies. Although PHMSA requires reporting of hazmat incidents through incident reporting forms, it does not require carriers to explicitly state on the form whether the incident is wetline-related. Consequently, to identify wetline incidents, PHMSA officials must review carrier-reported narratives and other information, a review that is resource-intensive. Moreover, this review may not result in an accurate accounting of the number and consequences of wetline incidents because the information does not always clearly indicate whether the incident is wetline-related and because of inaccuracies and omissions in the data. PHMSA has made efforts to improve its data, such as implementing quality checks, but this does not affect how wetline incidents are reported, and errors remain. This limits the usefulness of these data as supporting information for PHMSA's wetline regulatory analysis.

Limitations with PHMSA's Incident Data Make It Difficult to Identify Wetline Incidents

PHMSA's hazmat incident database does not specifically code incidents as wetline-related because its incident reporting form does not require carriers to explicitly report whether an incident is wetline-related. Consequently, it is not possible to retrieve a list of wetline incidents through PHMSA's database. To identify wetline incidents, PHMSA staff must analyze incident narratives and other carrier-reported information for characteristics that are indicative of wetline incidents.[14] This makes identifying these incidents resource-intensive and somewhat subjective, since the determination of which incidents are wetline-related is not always based on complete information, as incident data may be unclear or missing. OMB guidance states that agencies should develop a process for reviewing information quality as part of information resources management, including when collecting and maintaining the information to be used for regulatory analysis, which is one of PHMSA's uses for its incident data.

Wetline Incident Identification

Annually, PHMSA receives reports of about 15,000 to 20,000 hazmat incidents, and the percentage of these incidents that PHMSA identified as wetline-related is relatively small. To support PHMSA's 2011 cost-benefit analysis, PHMSA officials said that a team spent months reviewing incident data to identify wetline incidents and, as of January 2011, identified 172 wetline incidents occurring over the 10-year period from January 1999 through December 2008.[15] These incidents were used in the January 2011 proposed rule and related cost-benefit analysis. According to PHMSA's updated March 2012 draft cost-benefit analysis, after commenters in the wetline rulemaking docket questioned whether some of these incidents should have been identified as wetline incidents, PHMSA reexamined the 172 incidents it originally identified and updated the analysis to include incidents through March 2011. This led PHMSA to a provisional figure of 132 wetline incidents, which PHMSA used in its

---

[14]According to PHMSA's draft March 2012 regulatory analysis, a wetline incident is a reported incident meeting three criteria: 1) PHMSA can reasonably determine the incident involved damage or rupture to one or more of a cargo tank truck's wetlines; 2) flammable liquid was released; and 3) any reported fatalities, injuries, and damages were directly attributable to the release of product from the wetline.

[15]PHMSA's initial review to identify wetline incidents was conducted by a team of five or six people over the course of about 2 to 3 months. Although PHMSA did not track resources used to identify wetline incidents, officials said the process took about 10 minutes per incident reviewed and estimated the total effort between the initial review and a later review to identify incidents from 2009-2011 used about 1,200 staff hours.

updated 2012 draft cost-benefit analysis.[16] Because PHMSA has not issued a final rule on this subject, information in either the 2011 or draft 2012 analysis is subject to change.

To identify wetline incidents for both the 2011 and 2012 reviews, PHMSA officials said they conducted a broad search of cargo tank truck incidents in the database and then reviewed incident reports' narrative descriptions. If a description was insufficient to make a determination, officials reviewed the content of other fields in the incident's database entry such as component failure information, packaging identification, the amount and type of hazardous material released, and location of the vehicle at the time of the accident. PHMSA officials said their incident database provided sufficient information about incidents to make a judgment about each incident. However, the amount of time, staff, and specialized knowledge required for this process was more extensive than if PHMSA required carriers to identify whether incidents are wetline-related on the incident reporting forms. Officials also stated that, since their method of identifying wetline incidents by reviewing narrative descriptions required substantial resources, the agency was not able to direct additional resources to follow up with carriers to clarify missing or unclear data as part of the review to identify wetline incidents, except in cases involving fatalities.

In identifying consequences of wetline incidents, PHMSA has little information besides what is provided by the carriers. Specifically, only one wetline incident that occurred during the 1999 to 2011 incident study period was investigated by NTSB and PHMSA, and PHMSA officials said they were unaware of any other investigations of wetline incidents by

---

[16]In identifying incidents, PHMSA officials said they focused on those that would be affected by the proposed rule. For example, PHMSA cut 44 incidents from the original list of 172 identified incidents reported as involving a liquid release of greater than 50 gallons without a fire, under the assumption that since wetlines generally hold no more than 50 gallons of liquid, a spill of greater quantity would indicate a tank compartment breach or internal valve failure. In total, PHMSA cut 59 incidents from its original figure of 172 and added 19 new incidents from a review of incidents occurring from January 2009 through March 2011. There were less than 20 incidents in any given year from 1999-2011 that fall into this group of 132 wetline incidents. There were 16 incidents that involved fires and 7 that had one or more fatalities, which tended to involve occupants of the passenger vehicles.

federal, state, or local authorities during this period.[17] Therefore, PHMSA's record of the consequences of wetline incidents is based almost solely on information provided by carriers without corroborating information from other sources. Additionally, information provided by carriers is not always clear. For example, PHMSA officials said that carriers may misidentify components or use colloquialisms in the narrative (such as "fill tube" or "drop tube") to denote bottom lines. Further, officials said that terminology used in the report could vary depending on whether the carrier's corporate safety officer, the driver, or an attorney fills out the form.

PHMSA officials stated that they considered a number of factors in identifying wetline incidents for the 2011 proposed rule, such as characteristics that could indicate an incident was wetline-related in the absence of more definitive information and exceptions included in the proposed rule that would exclude certain incidents. For example, PHMSA officials told us they considered any tank truck incident involving a collision or crash with a fire to be a wetline incident, regardless of the amount of released flammable liquid.[18] The specific cause of incidents involving fires may be difficult to pinpoint, since the fire may destroy the forensic evidence needed to make that determination. Therefore, PHMSA officials assumed that incidents where the fire was not attributable to any one part of the vehicle were wetline-related because this approach would be less likely to exclude a severe incident that was caused by wetlines. However, this also means that the analysis could include severe incidents where the fire was the result of other factors, such as a puncture to the cargo tank. PHMSA officials stated that punctures to the cargo tank require forceful impact and are rare in incidents that do not involve a truck overturn. Therefore, in tank truck incidents with large spillages and fires, the fire likely began from the release of flammable liquid from bottom lines, according to PHMSA officials. Stakeholders disagree on whether this is a reasonable approach, with some supporting it because it can

---

[17]The investigated incident occurred in Pilesgrove, New Jersey in 2009. See NTSB, *Hazardous Materials Accident Brief, DCA-09-FZ-001* (Washington, D.C.: Nov. 12, 2009) and PHMSA, *Inspection/Investigation Report No. 09323047* (Landisville, N.J.: July 2, 2009). According to PHMSA officials, in 2012, the agency initiated a thorough review and follow-up audits of all incidents that resulted in death or injury, which officials believe will increase the likelihood of identifying wetline incidents.

[18]As previously discussed, wetlines hold a total of up to about 50 gallons of flammable liquid, so PHMSA excludes incidents reporting more than this amount that do not involve a fire.

address potential underreporting of incidents with fires and others stating that the practice artificially magnifies the benefits of the proposed regulation by including incidents that would not be prevented by eliminating wetlines.[19] In applying regulatory factors to the identification of wetline incidents, PHMSA excluded some incidents involving bottom line spillage due to exceptions in the proposed wetlines rule, such as incidents involving smaller trucks that the proposed rule would exclude from regulation.[20]

In determining whether particular incidents were wetline-related, PHMSA did not clearly document its decision-making process. For example, in reviewing incidents that occurred from 2009 to 2011, PHMSA identified 13 incidents as "possibly" wetline-related from the incident narrative information and subsequently used other incident information in making a final determination that 7 of those incidents were wetline-related.[21] Although officials documented these incidents in a spreadsheet, they did not include details about the specific decision-making process PHMSA used to make a final determination for each incident. Therefore, it is not clear how the agency concluded that 7 of the 13 "possibly" wetline-related incidents were wetline-related and that the other 6 incidents were not.

Incident Data Limitations

Our review of the reported incident data and narratives confirmed that it is challenging to identify wetline incidents. Using incident data other than the narratives, we attempted to identify wetline incidents on the basis of common characteristics of such incidents—involving a cargo tank truck, a release of flammable liquid, bottom line failure, and spillages or fires. In

---

[19]Industry stakeholders questioned whether any incident involving the release of more than 50 gallons of flammable liquid should be considered a wetline incident. PHMSA officials said they consider this legitimate because fires initiated by a wetline release could spread and compromise the main tank.

[20]The January 2011 proposed rule exempts smaller trucks, known as straight trucks, that are built with the cargo tank attached to the main truck rather than the larger truck-and-trailer style of truck as depicted in figure 1 because the truck's structure is assumed to provide sufficient protection for the wetlines.

[21]For example, PHMSA officials told us they identified a 2010 Portsmouth, Ohio, incident as wetline-related, despite the fact that its narrative description did not mention loading lines and its failure codes were left blank. Instead, PHMSA considered the type of vehicle (DOT-406 tank truck) and release amount (20-25 gallons) in the incident, which indicated to officials that this was a wetline incident since they believed a tank fracture would release much more product. Conversely, officials said that some incidents on the possibly wetline-related list were ruled out because, for example, their database entries indicated that wetlines were impacted but no release occurred.

doing so, we were unable to generate a list of incidents that approximated PHMSA's list of wetline incidents. Specifically, our search of the database turned up approximately 270 incidents from January 1999 through March 2011 that PHMSA did not identify as wetline-related because they involved driver error or spills from areas other than wetlines, among other reasons.[22] Conversely, some PHMSA-identified wetline incidents did not show up in our search results for reasons such as that they were coded as involving portable tanks instead of cargo tanks, indicating probable carrier error in reporting the incident.[23]

Additionally, inconsistencies with the component failure information in PHMSA's incident data limit the usefulness of this information for identifying wetline incidents. The incident reporting form has a field for carriers to report up to two components that were the most catastrophic failure points in the incident, such as reporting failure of the bottom lines.[24] PHMSA officials told us that although reporting this information is not optional, carriers sometimes leave this field blank, and the electronic version of the form lacks controls to force the entry of data in this field. Furthermore, carriers sometimes provide inaccurate information. For example, among the 132 incidents PHMSA identified as wetline-related, 99 of the database entries for those incidents either did not list a code indicating bottom-line failure or had blank codes.[25] PHMSA's guidance for filling out the incident reporting form includes a list of possible failure

---

[22]Our review does not suggest that these could possibly be wetline incidents; in fact, PHMSA officials pointed out reasons why such incidents could have other factors not easily detected in a cursory data review that would indicate they are not wetline incidents. As discussed in our report, because of limitations with how incidents are reported, PHMSA's process for identifying wetline incidents is resource-intensive and took months to complete for its regulatory analysis. A similar approach to identify wetline incidents was beyond our scope. Further, because of concerns about the reliability of PHMSA's data, we would not be able to independently identify wetline incidents without additional corroborating information.

[23]Under PHMSA regulations, portable tanks are not to transport hazardous materials unless they meet additional specifications. 49 C.F.R. § 173.32. In these instances, as PHMSA officials noted, it is likely that carriers misidentified the packaging type.

[24]Officials said the "loading/unloading line" and "inlet valve" codes, technically correspond to bottom lines, and carriers can use these codes to identify bottom line failure. However, as we discuss in the report, carriers use the codes in a minority of cases.

[25]For example, 77 PHMSA-identified wetline incidents indicated the "hose" or "piping/fitting" as the part that failed, terms that could refer to a range of other equipment, such as the hose a driver would use to deliver product to underground tanks at a gas station.

codes, but does not provide definitions of the codes. PHMSA officials said they do not have much confidence in using the failed components information for identifying wetline incidents. PHMSA officials acknowledged that missing data make it difficult to analyze incidents, but also said that the agency does not follow up with the carrier in these cases to confirm or correct the information unless the incident involves fatalities or injuries.[26]

Unclear Incident Narratives

Our review of the narratives for the 132 PHMSA-identified wetline incidents revealed that almost one-third of the narratives did not clearly identify the incidents as wetline-related because they lacked sufficient detail about the incident, used inconsistent terminology, or were blank. For example, some narratives indicated damage to other components that could have been the source of the spill. Other narratives did not indicate a collision resulting in a flammable liquid release. We also found instances of inconsistency in the database, such as narrative descriptions that did not corroborate other information provided in the database entry.[27] Table 1 shows the extent to which we were able to identify wetline incidents from the narratives.

---

[26]PHMSA officials said they are currently conducting a 6-month pilot test where staff are following up with carriers to obtain missing or inaccurate failure causes of tank truck hazmat incidents. However, according to PHMSA officials, it is not current agency policy to follow up on any fields other than fatalities and injuries. PHMSA officials said they conducted some follow up activity for all fatalities occurring in incidents cited in the draft March 2012 analysis.

[27]For example, the narrative for a 2010 Brighton, Colorado, incident reported a spill of over 135 gallons, but the field in the database indicated that the quantity released was 30 gallons.

Table 1: Extent That Narratives on PHMSA-Identified Wetline Incidents Clearly Characterized Incidents as Wetline-Related, January 1999 through March 2011

Extent that incidents were clearly wetline-related[a]	Number of incidents	Examples of incident descriptions[b]
Clearly wetline-related	93	• Bottom lines were impacted by a collision, causing a spill. The compartment above the line was not affected. • Bottom lines hit a post or pole at a gas station, causing a small release. • A passenger vehicle ran a red light and struck a trailer at the valves of the bottom lines, damaging the lines and resulting in a release and immediate fire.
Unclear if wetline-related	38	• The bottom line or internal valve leaked. • Bottom lines were damaged and minor tank damage also occurred. • A trailer struck an unattended vehicle. • A truck rolled over and gasoline spilled from the damaged trailer. • More than 50 gallons of liquid—the amount that would typically be in wetlines—were released from a tank truck after a collision. • Pipes froze and broke.
No narrative provided	1	
Total	**132**	

Source: GAO Analysis of PHMSA incident data.

[a]We assigned incidents to each category based on decision rules using PHMSA's definition of a wetline incident.

[b]Descriptions are paraphrased from actual incident narratives because carriers tended to use jargon and shorthand when describing the incidents.

Problems with PHMSA's Incident Data Limit Their Reliability for Regulatory Analysis, Even Though Improvement Efforts Have Been Taken

In addition to the limitations in identifying the number of incidents, we also found PHMSA's incident data inaccurately portray the consequences of wetline incidents, thus limiting their reliability for regulatory analysis. Internal control standards for federal executive branch agencies require that agencies have relevant, reliable, and timely information for decision-making and external reporting purposes.[28] OMB also has data quality guidelines for regulatory purposes.[29] Because much of the economic benefit of the proposed wetline regulation would be the avoided fatalities and damages from wetline incidents, inaccuracies in these data raise concerns about their reliability for accurately quantifying some benefits of the proposed rule. Specifically, we found problems with incident data related to fatalities and damages:

- Fatality Data. Among the 132 wetline incidents identified by PHMSA since 1999, there are 7 that PHMSA's incident data show had one or more fatalities, with a total of 11 fatalities.[30] However, the fatalities in 3 of the 7 incidents were misclassified as to whether they were caused by a hazmat release and thus preventable by the elimination of wetlines. According to PHMSA's incident-reporting guidance, hazmat-related deaths are directly attributed to the release of hazmat, such as a fatality caused by a fire resulting from the release of gasoline from wetlines. Nonhazmat-related deaths could occur in a hazmat incident but are attributed to other causes, such as internal injuries resulting from blunt force trauma during a collision. This distinction can have significant implications for the proposed rule's cost-benefit analysis. Since the avoidance of hazmat-related deaths is a major portion of the

---

[28]See, e.g., Federal Managers Financial Integrity Act of 1982, Pub. L. No. 97-255, 96 Stat. 814 (1982), and GAO, *Standards for Internal Control in the Federal Government*, GAO/AIMD 00 21.3.1 (Washington, D.C.: November 1999).

[29]Office of Management and Budget, *Regulatory Analysis, OMB Circular No. A-4* (Sept. 17, 2003). Circular A-4 states that federal agencies should assure compliance with OMB's "Guidelines for Ensuring and Maximizing the Quality, Objectivity, Utility, and Integrity of Information Disseminated by Federal Agencies" in their regulatory analyses. Those guidelines state that, among other things, agencies "shall adopt a basic standard of quality (including objectivity, utility, and integrity) as a performance goal and should take appropriate steps to incorporate information quality criteria into agency information dissemination practices."

[30]There is an additional 2000 Altoona, Pennsylvania, incident that the narrative says resulted in a fatality but that is not marked as such in the database fields that track fatalities. According to PHMSA's draft 2012 cost-benefit analysis, the fatality in this incident is nonhazmat-related. Although this incident does not affect the wetline cost-benefit analysis, it is another example of the inaccuracy of these data.

rule's calculated benefit, nonhazmat-related deaths are not included in the calculation as they would not be prevented by the rule. We found that fatalities in 2 of the 4 incidents recorded in PHMSA's database as hazmat-related were actually nonhazmat-related according to documentation about the incidents, which we confirmed with PHMSA officials.[31] Conversely, the fatality in 1 of the 3 incidents with fatalities recorded as nonhazmat-related was later determined to be hazmat-related.[32]

- Other Damage Data. Information on the dollar value of incident damages was sometimes missing or potentially inaccurate, since costs reported as "$0" in the database may represent no cost or an unreported cost.[33] PHMSA officials stated they have not always followed-up with carriers to obtain missing cost information and that carriers do not always have full cost information. Specifically, costs not incurred directly by carriers like response and cleanup costs may not be known to the carrier at the time of submitting the form.[34] Further, incidents with minor costs might not reflect any costs because carriers are not required to report total costs of $500 or less; however, in such cases, the data do not indicate whether a cost of $0 indicates an actual "no cost" that would not have to be reported or a greater cost that was unreported. Although carriers are expected to

---

[31]A 2001 Green Bay, Wisconsin, incident is recorded in the database as having four hazmat-related deaths, but PHMSA officials told us these fatalities were later determined to be nonhazmat-related. Additionally, a 2004 Taylor, Michigan, incident was originally recorded as having a hazmat-related fatality, but PHMSA recently changed its determination to a nonhazmat-related death and updated the database to reflect this.

[32]In this case, PHMSA's database showed the fatality in a 2009 Pilesgrove, New Jersey, wetline incident as nonhazmat-related, despite an NTSB investigation that determined the cause of the death to be a fire resulting from the release of flammable liquid from a tank truck's wetlines. After we discussed this with PHMSA officials, they amended the incident data and supporting documentation to state that the fatality was hazmat-related.

[33]The cost categories reportable to PHMSA are material loss (estimate of the cost of the product lost), carrier damage, property damage, response cost (including police and fire emergency response), and remediation (cleanup) cost. Cost fields marked as "$0" in the database could indicate the carrier reported it as blank (leaving a dash, or no value in the field) or as $0 in the original incident reporting form, making it impossible to tell whether the cost was unreported or actually $0.

[34]For example, for a 2004 incident in Taylor, Michigan, that involved a fire and a fatality, PHMSA officials said they made an attempt to confirm cleanup and property damage costs marked as "pending," but the carrier did not have this information and PHMSA did not make further attempts to follow up on the costs.

contact PHMSA with significant updates to cost estimates up to a year after reporting, officials stated that carriers often do not.

Concerns have been previously raised about the quality of PHMSA's incident data, including its usefulness for identifying wetline incidents. In a 2009 report on its data, PHMSA acknowledged the limitation that its wetline data analysis depends on reviewing narrative descriptions provided by carriers in reporting forms because wetline incidents are not specifically coded in the data.[35] Also that year, senior PHMSA officials' congressional testimony stated that identifying wetline incidents is staff-intensive and requires detailed analysis of database entries.[36] More recently, a 2013 National Academies Transportation Research Board report sponsored by PHMSA stated that detailed data on the nature of damages in incidents involving the release of hazardous materials are necessary for studying the performance of the container transporting the product. The report stated that while PHMSA's database collects some of this information, it is not sufficiently detailed.[37]

To address concerns about its data, PHMSA has made data process changes intended to improve the accuracy and completeness of its incident database. For example, PHMSA officials said that in 2012 the agency initiated a thorough review and follow-up audits of all incidents that result in deaths or injuries, which they said increases the likelihood of identifying wetline incidents. However, these changes do not address that wetline incidents are not specifically identified through the incident reporting process and do not apply to the inaccuracies in older incident

---

[35]PHMSA, *A Data Quality Assessment: Evaluating the Major Safety Data Programs for Pipeline and Hazardous Materials Safety* (Washington, D.C.: Nov. 10, 2009).

[36]*Reauthorization of the Department of Transportation's Hazardous Materials Safety Program, Hearing before the Subcommittee on Railroads, Pipelines and Hazardous Materials of the Committee on Transportation and Infrastructure, House of Representatives.* 111th Cong. 1 (May 2009) (statement of Cynthia Douglass, Acting Deputy Administrator, PHMSA, and Ted Willke, Associate Administrator, PHMSA)

[37]Transportation Research Board of the National Academies, *Feasibility Study for Highway Hazardous Materials Bulk Package Accident Performance Data Collection* (Washington, D.C.: 2013).

data. Some of the steps PHMSA has taken according to officials included the following:[38]

- In 2005, PHMSA updated its incident reporting form and process by, among other things, providing more specific options for identifying the part of the vehicle that failed and requiring carriers to submit report updates up to 1 year after an incident when information about incident fatalities or significant damages changes.

- Also in 2005, PHMSA implemented an electronic reporting option that incorporates checks to improve completeness before the form is approved in the database.[39]

- Since about 2 years ago, PHMSA has provided training and outreach to carriers on filling out the incident form more accurately and completely and to encourage online reporting.

- The agency implemented an improved data quality process starting in 2009, including updating its incident database to correct information it determined to be inaccurate. Before that time, the agency generally did not make changes to carrier-reported information in the system. Specifically, PHMSA reviews submitted incident reporting forms for accuracy and completeness and conducts follow-up with carriers to resolve missing information in the database.[40]

- To address concerns about under-reporting of incidents, PHMSA attempts to discover potentially reportable incidents by reviewing incident reports submitted to the National Response Center and

---

[38]PHMSA officials told us they are engaged in an ongoing effort to improve incident data in response to requirements in MAP-21, which they said includes conducting an assessment to review and improve the collection, analysis, reporting, and use of data related to accidents and incidents involving the transportation of hazmat, including better data on tank truck incidents. Officials indicated the efforts would not be completed by the publication date of this report. Therefore, we were unable to assess how this effort may improve data on wetline incidents.

[39]For example, if a carrier indicates on the form that the damages from the incident totaled over $500, the electronic reporting form will force the entry of a dollar value for at least one specific type of damage.

[40]However, PHMSA officials stated the improvements are not retroactive to incidents occurring before 2005.

monitoring the news media.[41] PHMSA tracks severe incidents that may need reporting by carriers and, if warranted, may contact the carrier to request submittal of a reporting form, a process that has identified some wetline incidents, according to PHMSA officials.

- In an effort to improve the accuracy of its fatality and injury data, PHMSA developed a worksheet to better track and confirm information about fatalities and injuries.[42] In 2012, PHMSA began working with the Federal Motor Carriers Safety Administration to investigate hazmat incidents involving fatalities, injuries, and fires. Also in 2012, PHMSA began retaining coroner's or medical examiner's reports associated with each fatality.[43]

Although these efforts could improve PHMSA's incident data going forward, they have no effect on some of PHMSA's older wetline incident data. The agency relied on data back to 1999 in analyzing costs and benefits of its proposed wetline rule. As previously discussed, upon reexamination of its data, PHMSA changed the number of wetline incidents supporting its current proposed rule. However, because of the subjective nature of how wetline incidents are identified, the possibility still exists that PHMSA's identification of some incidents as wetline-related may be inaccurate. Industry stakeholders told us they believe PHMSA's data overstate the prevalence of wetline incidents and that their low number does not justify regulation. Conversely, some safety stakeholders said such incidents may be underreported. Additionally, as we have mentioned earlier, we found inaccuracies in these data, limiting their reliability for accurately quantifying the consequences of wetline incidents. In particular, flaws with the fatality and damages data have the potential to skew calculations of the rule's benefit of avoiding wetline-related

---

[41]Federal regulation requires notification to the National Response Center in the event of a hazardous material incident that meets specific criteria such as involving a fatality, an evacuation of the general public, or a shutdown of a transportation artery for 1 hour or more. See 49 C.F.R. § 171.15.

[42]The Death and Injury summary is a worksheet for PHMSA internal purposes in which staff record information confirmed each time they contact carriers. This is part of PHMSA's overall quality control process for hazmat incident data.

[43]Although PHMSA officials said they have always reviewed these reports, the agency did not retain them prior to 2012 because of concerns about retaining personally identifiable information. More recently, the agency decided to begin retaining the reports under lock and key whereby interested parties might be provided redacted versions or information about the sources PHMSA obtained the reports from.

fatalities. This calls into question whether these data are sufficiently reliable to support regulatory analysis unless PHMSA makes adjustments for the potential uncertainty in the analysis. Without accurate data on the number and consequences of wetline incidents, the consequences of wetline incidents remain unclear and the benefits of wetlines regulation may not be accurately calculated in PHMSA's regulatory analysis.

Stakeholders Identified Existing and Potential Options to Address Wetline Risks, but Have Concerns about Safety, Costs, and Implementation

An Existing Purging System to Address Wetline Safety Risks Is in Limited Use

A purging system is a device a carrier or manufacturer can install on a cargo tank truck that removes liquid from the truck's bottom lines after a driver finishes loading the cargo tanks at the fuel terminal. One company, Cargo Tank Concepts, manufactures a purging system that uses compressed air from an auxiliary tank to push the liquid in the bottom lines through small ancillary lines and into the cargo compartments (see fig. 5). When the purge is complete, the lines retain only residual amounts of liquid and vapor.

Figure 5: The Main Components of Cargo Tank Concepts' Automatic Wetline Purging System

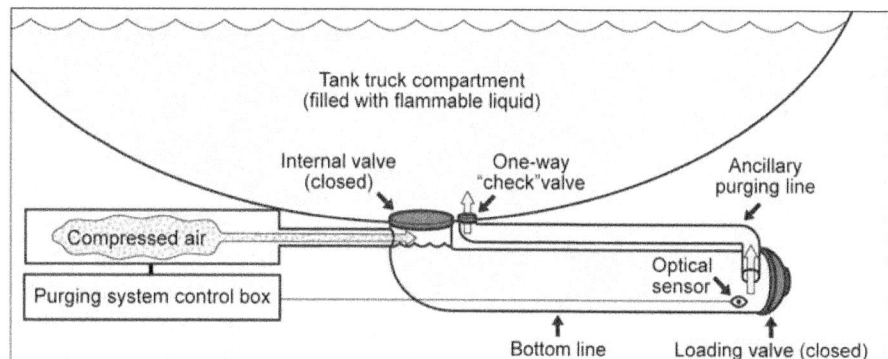

The **purging system control box** is alerted by an **optical sensor** when liquid needs to be purged from the **bottom line**. With the **internal valve** and **loading valve** closed, **compressed air** is introduced into the bottom line, which displaces the liquid out through the **ancillary purging line**, a **one-way check valve**, and back into the **tank truck compartment**.

Source: GAO analysis and observance of Cargo Tank Concepts' technology.

Cargo Tank Concepts designed two versions of the purging system: automatic and manual. With the automatic system, after the driver finishes loading the cargo tank, electronic sensors detect liquid in the bottom lines and the system automatically begins to purge. One major petroleum company installed the automatic purging system on its cargo tank truck fleet starting in the late 1990s.[44] Cargo Tank Concepts has also equipped a few trucks owned by other carriers with the automatic version to demonstrate the purging system. The manual system engages when the driver pushes a button to activate the purge, typically after loading the cargo tank. According to the purging system manufacturer, as of June 2013, there were no manual purging systems in use.[45] PHMSA officials, three industry stakeholders, and two safety stakeholders told us that they anticipate other purging solutions would be developed if PHMSA's

---

[44]The company is a terminal operator, carrier, and marketer. It transports and stores petroleum, operates terminals, and sells fuel at thousands of retail outlets.

[45]Cargo Tank Concepts told us in June 2013 that a carrier had contacted the company about purchasing and installing a manual system soon.

proposed wetlines rule were to go into effect.[46] We contacted two other manufacturers that an industry publication reported were developing wetline purging systems. Both companies told us they have not produced any systems other than prototypes; however, both said they could move forward with development, and eventually production, if PHMSA finalizes a wetlines rule.

Industry associations and companies, manufacturers, repair shops, federal agencies, and safety groups identified advantages and disadvantages of using a purging system to address wetline risks. Due to limited use, most stakeholders do not have first-hand experience with the wetline purging system and its performance. Thus, stakeholders' familiarity with the more technical aspects of the system varied and some stakeholders, particularly safety groups, declined to comment. However, based on their expertise with cargo tank trucks and transporting flammable liquids, stakeholders provided views on using such a system in that operating environment.

According to stakeholders, the advantages of using a purging system include:

- Addressing wetline safety risks: Purging removes all but a residual amount of liquid from the bottom lines, in accordance with one of the ways to meet the standard in PHMSA's proposed rule. Removing flammable liquid from the bottom lines may reduce fatalities and the number and severity of injuries in the event of a broad-side collision between a passenger vehicle and a cargo tank truck. The absence of liquid in the bottom lines may also reduce property and environmental damages associated with hazardous materials spilling from the bottom lines.

- Identifying faulty valves: Depending on the design of a purging system, it may permit detection of faulty internal emergency valves. If an emergency valve is not working properly, liquid may leak from a cargo tank compartment into the bottom lines. In the event of a collision with wetlines, a faulty emergency valve could cause a carrier

---

[46]Between January 1999 and January 2013, at least six patent applications for technologies to address wetline safety risks were filed with the U.S. Patent Office. Three of these applications, all granted, were for systems to purge wetlines, while two others were for systems designed to reduce the amount of liquid spilled in the event that a bottom line shears off from the cargo tank.

to lose liquid from an entire cargo tank compartment. If a purging system attempts to purge liquid when the line should be clear, a driver may be alerted that there is a problem; if the driver were not alerted, the faulty valve could go undetected until the next inspection.

Stakeholders also raised a number of concerns about purging systems, but disagreed about the significance of them:

- Retrofitting: Industry stakeholders are concerned about the safety of installing purging systems on in-service tank trucks due to the risk that welding on the tanks—if not completely free of gasoline vapor—creates a risk of explosion. Specifically, 9 industry stakeholders and 3 safety groups we interviewed raised this issue, and 18 of the 21 of the industry associations and companies providing comment in response to PHMSA's 2011 proposed wetlines rule reinforced those concerns as being a risk if the proposed regulation required retrofitting.[47] However, stakeholders also acknowledged that there are procedures that allow welding to be done safely, and repair shops routinely weld on cargo tanks when they require repair. Cargo Tank Concepts did not characterize the concern about retrofitting as significant, but the company has developed a "nonwelded" alternative to address industry concerns, which it has installed on one truck. However, three industry stakeholders expressed concern about the durability of such an installation, two of whom added that the "nonwelded" alternative would still entail "hotwork" such as cutting into the tank.[48] According to Cargo Tank Concepts, the nonwelded installation involves drilling but not cutting, welding or other types of "hotwork."

- Installation time: Stakeholders' estimates on the amount of time needed to install a purging system on an existing tank truck varied from 8 to 40 hours. While Cargo Tank Concepts provided the lowest estimate of 8 hours, an industry stakeholder with firsthand experience

---

[47]The extent that the proposed rule would require retrofitting depends on how much time the industry would be given to comply, with a shorter compliance period requiring more retrofitting than a longer one in which existing vehicles could be replaced by new ones that already have a purging system installed by the manufacturer.

[48]In assessing the feasibility of the purging system technology, PHMSA officials told us they observed the function of a prototype model of the purging system that was not installed on an actual cargo tank truck. Thus, PHMSA has not assessed the feasibility of the nonwelded installation, although officials told us they believed such construction techniques were in keeping with other aspects of cargo tank truck manufacturing.

installing a purging system estimated that installation takes from 30 to 34 hours of labor. The higher estimates include time to "de-gas" the cargo tank to reduce risk of explosion, increasing the cost of installation compared to that on new cargo tanks since those would not need to be de-gassed. PHMSA's regulatory assessment that considers different timeframes for implementing a wetlines rule assumes such retrofitting could be done concurrent with 5-year interval inspections, which involve de-gassing the tank.

- Delays: An industry analysis of PHMSA's proposed regulation and six industry stakeholders suggest that use of the purging system could delay drivers at fuel terminals, potentially causing backlogs, while others said that the purging system will not delay drivers because it can operate while drivers are completing necessary final steps before leaving a fuel terminal. One industry stakeholder said that the purging system would lengthen unloading times, since the system uses the truck's air compressor thereby lowering the pressure available for facilitating unloading and slowing unloading speeds. According to Cargo Tank Concepts, the system uses very little air, and air that is used is replaced quickly by the air compressor and therefore would have no impact on unloading.

- Vapor release: Because purging systems use air to push liquid into the tank, the systems increase the pressure in the tank. In 2005, the California Air Resources Board expressed concern that this increase would exceed the tank's design limit, causing it to vent gasoline vapor into the air potentially in violation of emissions limits, a concern echoed by one industry stakeholder we interviewed and in nine comments submitted in response to PHMSA's proposed regulation.[49] However, according to Cargo Tank Concepts, the increase in air pressure is too small to trigger the pressure release valves and cause such release.

- Malfunction: Since PHMSA's proposed rule prohibits wetlines without adequate collision protection, in the event of a purging system malfunction, a truck would likely not be able to leave a terminal unless it could purge its bottom lines. One industry stakeholder was unsure

---

[49]The American Petroleum Institute, the American Trucking Associations, the Truck Trailer Manufacturers Association, the Dangerous Goods Advisory Council, and Baltimore Cargo Tank Services referenced the California Air Resources Board's concerns in their written comments.

how carriers would address the issue of potential malfunction of a purging system, but speculated that the truck would have to be off-loaded, potentially to another truck or, if the truck was at a fuel terminal, via an off-loading station. PHMSA officials said it might be possible to create a regulatory exception to allow one-time movement of the cargo to its unloading destination or to transfer the cargo to a different truck. In either case, the truck with a faulty system could then not be reloaded until after the purging system is repaired. Cargo Tank Concepts also noted that in the event of a purging system malfunction, only the product in the bottom lines would have to be removed, not the entire contents of the tank.

- Maintenance: Industry stakeholders agree that the purging system would result in additional maintenance and repair costs to the carrier. In comments submitted to PHMSA in response to the proposed rule, six industry stakeholders expressed concerns about the unknown cost of maintenance and repair of the purging system, as well as the absence of data on factors such as maintenance, reliability, down-time, and repair and replacement costs. Two industry stakeholders we interviewed expressed concern that extreme operating conditions—very cold or hot climates, for example—could affect the system and therefore maintenance costs. However, according to one industry stakeholder familiar with the system, issues with the purging system are fairly easy to address. Cargo Tank Concepts commented that they have sold hundreds of purging systems that are operating reliably and incur low maintenance costs.

- Compliance: Four industry stakeholders said that compliance with PHMSA's proposed regulation could be an issue for carriers. One of those stakeholders said this could be a particular issue with the manual purging system that required drivers to proactively initiate purging, as some drivers may forget to initiate the purge, while others may skip purging to save time. Additionally, that stakeholder suggested that drivers may have a disincentive to purge bottom lines if using the vehicle's compressed air system for that purpose reduced the efficiency of other truck operations. Furthermore, according to two stakeholders, it could be difficult for carriers or third parties to verify compliance, given that some bottom lines lack glass panes that allow visual verification of the amount of liquid present in the bottom line. PHMSA officials did not view this as a major concern and told us that regulatory compliance cannot always be fully monitored. PHMSA also noted that carriers could choose other methods of eliminating wetlines besides the purging system.

Other Options to Address Wetline Safety Risks Are Not in Use, and Many Are Hypothetical

Stakeholders identified other options to address wetline safety risks in addition to the purging system. However, none of the other options are in use by the industry and many are hypothetical, making it is difficult to assess their costs, benefits, and feasibility. DOT summarized a number of options to address wetline safety risks in a 1999 preliminary cost-benefit analysis, but additional information about options other than the purging system was limited to propositions and conjecture.[50] Therefore, we relied on views from industry and safety stakeholders to determine the advantages and disadvantages of each option. Table 2 summarizes options and key advantages and disadvantages as identified by stakeholders.

Table 2: Stakeholders' Views on Options to Address Wetline Risks

Options	Description	Advantages	Disadvantages
Purging system installed on the cargo tank truck	After loading, system introduces compressed air from an auxiliary tank into the wetlines under low pressure, pushing liquid from the wetlines into the cargo tank body.	Eliminates all but trace amounts of fuel from bottom lines. May detect internal valve leaks. Retrofit feasible. Currently in use.	If malfunctioning, other measures would be needed to empty wetlines. Driver compliance with manual system difficult for carriers to enforce. Opinions varied on consequences of low pressurization of an unpressurized tank. Significant concern from industry over dangers of welding work needed for this option if DOT were to require retrofitting.
Purging system installed at the loading terminals	After loading, the driver would connect to a stationary purging system. The system would then introduce air into the wetlines, forcing liquid from the wetlines into the cargo tank body.	Eliminates all but trace amounts of fuel from bottom lines. May help detect leaks in cargo tank internal emergency valves. Retrofit feasible.	Adds to time the driver spends at the terminal. Difficult for carriers to enforce. Requires modification to both trucks and terminals.
Short loading lines	Shorter loading lines are added to tank trucks so that bottom lines are used only for unloading.	Reduces the amount of liquid in external lines. Lines would not be exposed to damage in the event of a rollover.	Retrofit infeasible. Greater distance between loading heads would necessitate modifications to either the loading rack or loading procedure, raising some cost and safety concerns.

[50]U.S. Department of Transportation, Research and Special Programs Administration, *Risk / Benefit-Cost Analysis, Prohibiting Hazardous Material in External Piping of MC 306 / DOT 406 Cargo Tank Motor Vehicles: Preliminary Assessment* (Washington, D.C.: 1999).

Options	Description	Advantages	Disadvantages
Internal lines	The horizontal components of bottom lines would be placed on the inside of tank compartments.	Eliminates liquid in external lines. Minimizes exposed elements	Retrofit infeasible. Loading line leaks would no longer be visible and may contaminate liquid.
Double-closing stop valve	Upon collision, a self-closing stop valve would protect against cargo tank spills while other closures would seal wetline ends.	Reduces risk that designed-to-fail shear point will result in flammable liquid spill. Retrofit feasible.	Does not eliminate wetlines. Stop valve could be damaged in the event of a collision. To reduce wetline risk further would require stronger pipes, like the protection of tanks for trucks carrying propane.
Top loading	Cargo tank trucks would be loaded from the top of the tank.	Eliminates liquid in external lines.	Modifications necessary to meet vapor recovery requirements, address issues of worker safety. Requires reconfiguration of loading racks.
Draining wetlines at the terminal	After loading the truck and closing the valves the carrier would reconnect to a tank (either at the rack or elsewhere in the terminal) and drain the liquid in the bottom lines.	Eliminates liquid in external lines. Terminals currently have storage tanks for "slop."	Terminals would need new administrative processes, revised automated metering, and additional storage—possibly separate storage unit for each liquid. Mixing products would inhibit resale; if unable to be sold, would create hazardous waste.
Guards, shields, or under-ride protection	Cargo tank trucks would be equipped with bottom damage protection devices.	Reduces risk of wetline rupture.	Does not eliminate wetlines. Retrofit inadvisable, possibly infeasible. Added weight of guards would reduce the carrying capacity of tank trucks. In a collision, the guards could puncture the tank or transfer force and cause the tank to rupture. Guards to prevent pedestrian and bicycle under-rides would not sufficiently protect the tank.

Source: GAO analysis of documents from DOT's 2004 and 2011 proposed regulations to address wetline safety risk, as well as interviews with PHMSA, NTSB, Cargo Tank Concepts, industry stakeholders, and safety groups.

For all the options, the most obvious advantage is the potential to address wetline safety risks, but according to stakeholders, the extent that these options address those risks varies. Some options would leave traces of fuel in the cargo tank trucks' bottom lines, while others would retain wetlines but potentially reduce risk by shielding them or altering wetline design to minimize spillage in the event of a collision.

Some stakeholders' concerns with the wetline purging system apply to other options as well, such as concerns about the safety of retrofitting cargo tank trucks. For at least three of the other options, retrofits are either not feasible or inadvisable, which would mean these options could only be implemented on new tank trucks, delaying safety benefits. In addition, the entity that would bear the initial cost of implementation varies among the options. For example, one stakeholder said that carriers would bear the initial cost of installing side-guards on tank trucks to shield them from collisions, since that option would require changes to the cargo tank design. In contrast, short loading lines that would replace the longer bottom lines for loading tanks could require changes to the cargo tank design and modifications to the loading rack, so the carriers and the fuel terminals would both incur initial costs. Stakeholders suggested that other agencies, such as the Environmental Protection Agency or the Occupational Safety and Health Administration, may need to be consulted on the design and implementation of some options due to potential environmental and/or worker-safety concerns.

PHMSA Analyzed Costs and Benefits for a Proposed Wetlines Rule, but Uncertainties Limit the Usefulness of the Analysis

PHMSA Proposed a Rule to Address Wetline Safety Risks and Analyzed Associated Costs and Benefits

In January 2011, PHMSA issued a notice of proposed rulemaking to prohibit the transport of flammable liquid in the bottom lines of cargo tank trucks unless the vehicle is equipped with bottom damage protection devices, along with an analysis of the proposal's costs and benefits. In March 2012, PHMSA updated the assumptions of its cost-benefit analysis in response to comments submitted by stakeholders in the rulemaking and also changed its methodology (for discussion of the changed methodology, see app. II). We reviewed the assumptions and methodology in the March 2012 working draft document because they reflected PHMSA's more current thinking; however, this document was provided in draft form and has not been released publicly. PHMSA has not issued a final rule on this subject; therefore, information in either the 2011 or 2012 analysis is subject to change. PHMSA officials told us they ceased all work on the rulemaking in response to the MAP-21 requirement that PHMSA not issue a final rule pending the completion of our study. PHMSA may, however, issue a rule earlier if it determines that a risk to public safety, property, or the environment is present or an imminent hazard exists and that the regulation will address the risk or hazard.

PHMSA based its cost-benefit analysis on the assumption that the industry would comply with the proposed rule by installing a wetline purging system on cargo tank trucks—specifically the manual version of the system offered by Cargo Tank Concepts.[51] PHMSA's analysis included multiple compliance scenarios that varied in the amount of time the industry would have to comply with the rule. The longest scenario called for compliance within 20 years, which, given PHMSA's assumption that tank trucks have a 20-year life, would mean the device could be installed on only new trucks and no retrofitting would be needed. The shortest scenario called for compliance within 5 years and assumed the industry would retrofit many of its existing tank trucks concurrently with a truck's required 5-year inspection, at which time PHMSA officials told us trucks are cleaned of gasoline and vapor as part of the inspection process, reducing the risk of explosion from welding on an existing tank.

PHMSA's 2011 analysis found that costs exceeded benefits in all of the compliance scenarios, while the 2012 analysis concluded that benefits exceeded costs on a present value basis by about $2 million in the 20-year scenario; but costs exceeded benefits in the three scenarios with shorter compliance time frames. Table 3 describes the costs and benefits considered in the analysis.

---

[51]Although the proposed rule states compliance could be achieved by installing specified types of bottom damage protection, stakeholders told us this option is possibly infeasible and retrofits would be inadvisable for tank trucks (see previous table 2). PHMSA's cost-benefit analysis does not consider costs and benefits of bottom protection as a compliance option.

Table 3: Costs and Benefits Included in PHMSA's 2011 Cost-Benefit Analysis and Its 2012 Draft Revision

Costs	Benefits
• Purchase and installation of manual wetline purging systems on all cargo tank trucks. • Annual maintenance of purging systems. • Weight penalty, resulting from the reduced carrying capacity of a tank truck to account for the weight of the purging system.[a] • For the 2012 analysis, PHMSA also included additional operating costs that carriers would incur to transport product displaced by the added weight of the purging system.	• Avoidance of all wetline incidents, including associated fatalities, product loss, clean-up costs, carrier damage, and property damage. (The 2011 analysis also included evacuation delays, but this was removed in the 2012 analysis.) • Avoidance of associated consequences, such as traffic delays and risk to emergency responders. • Avoidance of a low-probability, high-consequence event such as the 1997 Yonkers incident.

Source: GAO analysis of PHMSA's 2011 cost-benefit analysis and 2012 working draft cost-benefit analysis.

[a]Federal regulation limits the weight of commercial vehicles on the interstate highway system, see 23 C.F.R. part 658. In general, off the interstate highway system, states may set their own commercial vehicle weight standards. Therefore, the added weight of a purging system could result in decreased product carrying capacity.

PHMSA withdrew a previous proposed wetlines rule in 2006 because it determined that the rule's potential benefits did not justify its costs. The agency issued its more recent proposal in 2011 because the agency still views preventing wetline incidents as an important safety issue and, according to PHMSA officials, given further development of the wetline purging system, preventing wetline incidents can now be done in a manner that is cost-beneficial. In contrast, 11 of the 12 industry stakeholders we spoke with opposed the proposed rule for reasons such as their belief that wetlines are not a major safety issue and their concerns about the possible solutions, which were previously discussed in this report.[52] Six of the 10 safety stakeholders we interviewed supported the rule, while three others took no position. Four other safety groups we contacted declined to be interviewed because they had no position on the issue.

---

[52]One industry stakeholder, a petroleum marketer and carrier that uses the wetline purging system, told us it has no position on the proposed regulation.

Uncertainty Associated with Aspects of PHMSA's Cost-Benefit Analysis Limits Its Usefulness for Supporting the Proposed Rule

OMB has issued guidance for agencies engaged in rulemaking on the use of data and treatment of uncertainty in cost-benefit analysis.[53] The guidance states that market data is a rich source of information, and that estimating cost when active markets do not exist is more difficult, requiring appropriate proxies. Accordingly, an agency should discuss the quality of available data used and in the absence of adequate data, the agency will need to make certain assumptions. With regard to uncertainty, the guidance states that estimates of benefits and costs are typically uncertain because of imprecision in underlying data and assumptions. Because uncertainty is common when conducting cost-benefit analysis, OMB states that the effects of uncertainty should be analyzed and reported. To address plausible changes in the assumptions and numeric inputs of a cost-benefit analysis, OMB recommends that agencies consider providing a sensitivity analysis to show how the results of the analysis might vary to account for such uncertainty. Limitations of the analysis because of uncertainty or biases surrounding data or assumptions should, according to OMB, be discussed. Additionally, the OMB guidance provides that when uncertainty has significant effects on the final conclusion about net benefits, the agency should consider additional research prior to rulemaking.

PHMSA's calculated benefits are based on the assumption that use of the purging system by tank truck carriers will prevent all wetline incidents; the value of this benefit is based on PHMSA's analysis of its past incident data to identify wetline incidents and their associated consequences. Other assumptions in the analysis are based on testimonial information and observation, rather than market data. Specifically, cost calculations are based on information from the purging system's manufacturer regarding the purchase and installation costs of the technology. Additionally, information about purging system performance—an input that can affect both benefits and costs—is based on 1) information from the manufacturer, 2) anecdotal information about the performance of the technology provided by the major carrier that is using the automatic version of the system, and 3) PHMSA's observation of a prototype version of the manual purging system that shows how the technology works but is not actually installed on a tank truck. Although PHMSA included sensitivity analyses in its 2011 and 2012 cost-benefit analyses to account for some uncertainties, issues with the data and assumptions

---

[53]Office of Management and Budget, *Guidelines and Discount Rates for Benefit Cost Analysis of Federal Programs*, OMB Circular A-94, (revised 1992), and *Regulatory Analysis,* OMB Circular A-4, (Sept. 17, 2003).

that can affect costs and benefits were not addressed through sensitivity analysis.[54] Consequently, some costs and benefits in the analysis may be more uncertain than PHMSA has accounted for.

Cost Assumptions

PHMSA's analysis assumes a cost of $2,300 to equip each new or existing cargo tank truck with a manual wetline purging system, plus the cost of installation labor, rather than the higher cost of the automatic version currently used, which the manufacturer sells for $3,800 or $3,950 depending on the size of the tank truck.[55] PHMSA assumed companies would opt for the manual system because of its lower cost and used that as the cost basis in its analysis. As previously discussed, there are no manual systems in use to date, and some industry stakeholders suggested that carriers may prefer the automatic system for compliance and simplicity reasons, despite its higher cost. Thus, although there is a limited market for the automatic purging system, the lack of market use to date for the manual system makes the cost of compliance with the regulation uncertain despite a stated price from the manufacturer.

Were the proposed rule issued, such action would likely generate demand for the purging technology, which could have several effects. Specifically, it could enable the product to be produced at a lower cost due to achieving economies of scale related to a higher level of production, and it could also attract more companies into the market to produce alternative purging systems. Although we are aware of only one company offering purging system technology at the time of our review, at

---

[54]PHMSA included sensitivity analyses to test how costs and benefits could differ if certain of the assumptions were changed. In the 2011 sensitivity analysis, costs were tested with alternative assumptions of a lower purging system installation cost and no additional costs related to the weight of the purging unit, assumptions which lowered the proposed rule's cost. Costs were also tested with an assumption of a greater number of equipped trucks, an assumption that would increase cost. Additionally, benefits were tested under an alternative assumption of a higher number of avoided fatalities and other damages—changes that would increase the proposed rule's benefit. The 2012 analysis included two sensitivity calculations: a "bunching" analysis, which assumed carriers would equip their trucks with the technology as late as possible to meet the compliance deadline, and an alternative assumption about the price of the purging system being lower than assumed in the base case, due to the manufacturer's reduction in the price of the manual wetline purging system.

[55]PHMSA used the $2,300 cost because it was the price Cargo Tank Concepts offered the manual purging system at until the company more recently dropped its listed price to $1,380. PHMSA's draft 2012 analysis acknowledges the price drop and included a sensitivity analysis to test the effect of a lower-cost purging system. PHMSA officials told us they did the calculations with the higher value to be more conservative.

least three patents for other purging systems have been granted, making industry competition a possibility. Consequently, in the absence of market-based information for the manual purging system, it is difficult to develop assumptions on the cost of the technology for the cost-benefit analysis. While these factors could have an impact on the sales price of the unit, PHMSA's analysis does not fully account for these cost uncertainties and, to the extent that market information exists for the automatic purging system, such information is not used to support costs in the analysis. PHMSA's analysis presents a sensitivity analysis only for a lower cost of the purging system on the basis that a more competitive market could develop if its proposed rule were finalized and that the manufacturer recently began offering the manual purging system at a lower price.

Additionally, stakeholders we spoke with mentioned a number of other cost-related concerns:

- Installation approach. As previously discussed, stakeholders raised safety concerns about potential welded retrofitting needed to install purging systems under the shorter compliance scenarios, due to the risk of explosion if cargo tanks are not thoroughly de-gassed. Safety measures to address these concerns could add additional cost. However, PHMSA's analysis addressed these concerns by stating that carriers could install nonwelded purging systems. PHMSA officials also told us that because the compliance scenarios were created with 5-year intervals, retrofitting could occur concurrently with 5-year inspections when tanks are normally cleared of flammable product and vapor. PHMSA officials also stated that there are procedures to de-gas tanks to make them safe for such work.

- Installation time. PHMSA's analysis does not include the cost of down-time to install the purging system, even for scenarios requiring retrofitting because the analysis assumes the work can be done concurrently with routine inspections. However, stakeholders reported a range of time needed to install a purging system, which could take longer than the inspections; thus it is unclear that the inspection and retrofitting could actually be done simultaneously.

- Maintenance. PHMSA assumes maintenance on a purging system will cost $3 per year per truck, based on an assumption about the cost of inspecting the device every 5 years. Stakeholders with experience using the technology said this cost is too low and told us the technology required occasional repairs or replacement. According to PHMSA's analysis, it includes a low-cost maintenance estimate because it states that pneumatic technologies like the purging system require very little maintenance because they have few moving parts that can fail.

We also found uncertainty in PHMSA's data and assumptions related to benefits:

- Fatalities. As previously discussed, we identified inaccuracies in PHMSA's analysis regarding the number of fatalities that could be avoided by the proposed wetlines rule, and PHMSA did not include a sensitivity analysis to account for its rule potentially preventing fewer deaths than assumed in its cost-benefit analysis. Both the 2011 and 2012 cost-benefit analyses stated there were 4 incidents with hazmat-related fatalities during the incident study period (resulting in 5 fatalities).[56] After discussing the inaccuracies with PHMSA officials, they agreed it would be more accurate for their analysis to reflect 4 fatalities occurring from 3 fatal wetline incidents. Questions over PHMSA's wetline fatality analysis have been raised before. In a 2001 letter critiquing a prior wetlines proposed rule, OMB encouraged DOT to more fully address the uncertainty in the cause of fatalities in its wetlines cost-benefit analysis, specifically to address uncertainty with whether fatalities might be caused by factors other than the release of hazardous materials and would therefore not be avoided by a rule addressing wetlines.

  Because fatalities are a major contributor to the calculated value of the benefits of the regulation, a reduction of even one fatality in the analysis could have significant impact on the amount of calculated benefits for the proposed rule.[57] For example, PHMSA's 2012 analysis concluded that with 4 fatal incidents during the study period and an average of 1.67 people per vehicle, the proposed rule would

---

[56]Although there were additional wetline incidents during this period with fatalities, those fatalities were attributed to causes other than the release of hazmat, such as blunt force trauma, and thus are not counted as contrbuting to the benefits of the proposed wetline rule.

[57]For calculating the benefits of proposed rules that seek to prevent the loss of life, DOT uses a value of statistical life that seeks to represent the benefit of preventing a fatality. Specifically, the statistical value of one life is the amount that society is willing to pay for a safety improvement that would prevent one fatality. PHMSA's draft 2012 analysis used a value of $6.2 million that DOT set in 2011. More recently, in 2013, DOT revised the value of statistical life to be $9.1 million in 2012 dollars.

GAO-13-721 Cargo Tank Trucks

avoid 6.7 fatalities for a benefit of about $3.4 million per year.[58] Were the analysis recalculated with 3 fatal incidents, the annual benefit of avoided fatalities would be about $2.5 million per year, about $1 million less. This is significant, given that avoided fatalities comprise more than half of the almost $6.5 million total annual benefit of the proposed rule. In the 2012 draft cost-benefit analysis, PHMSA's 20-year compliance scenario showed a total net benefit of about $2 million, which was the only scenario where benefits exceeded costs. Thus, while PHMSA has not issued a final rule on this subject and information in either the 2011 or draft 2012 analysis is subject to change, had the analysis been calculated with one less fatal incident, costs would have exceeded benefits in that scenario as well.

- <u>Effectiveness</u>. PHMSA's analysis assumes its proposed rule would prevent all wetline incidents, implying that the purging systems installed to prevent these incidents would be 100 percent effective. However, PHMSA's analysis does not acknowledge that the system may malfunction, may not prevent wetline incidents due to certain intervening factors, and that the system may not always be used as intended. We are aware of two wetline incidents that have occurred since 2008 involving trucks equipped with an automatic wetline purging system. According to the carrier involved in both incidents, in one instance, the driver had turned off the system and, in the other, a problem with the lining of the cargo tank prevented the system from functioning properly. Based on this information, it does not appear there was a functional problem with the purging device in either instance; however, wetline incidents occurred nonetheless.

- <u>Most Catastrophic Incident</u>. PHMSA's 2011 and 2012 analyses included additional benefits from avoiding a low-probability, high-consequence event like the 1997 Yonkers incident. Even though the Yonkers incident occurred prior to the years for which data were used for the primary analysis of expected benefits, this incident was included in the analysis—meaning that it comprised a portion of the

---

[58]In the 2011 analysis, avoided fatalities were about $3.9 million of the more than $7.7 million in annual expected consequences and would also be about $1 million less per year if calculated with one less fatal incident. Figures are in 2009 dollars. The numbers of fatalities and fatal incidents did not change between the 2011 and 2012 versions of the cost-benefit analysis. Because the 2012 analysis covered a longer period of time, the benefit per year of avoided fatalities was lower in the updated analysis. PHMSA's assumptions about the number of passengers per car and the statistical value of a life were also slightly different in both analyses.

expected benefits due to accidents avoided—under the assumption that a severe incident such as this would happen very infrequently. Specifically, in both of these analyses, the expected benefits of avoiding an incident of this level of consequence were allocated over a 20-year period—meaning that the agency assumed such a catastrophic incident could be expected to occur once every 20 years. PHMSA officials told us they considered allocating the benefits over a longer 40-year period in response to industry criticism that there has been only one such extraordinary incident on record but that the agency has not reached a final decision on this issue. When assumed to be a 20-year event, the expected benefits of avoiding a Yonkers-like incident in the 2012 benefit cost analysis comprise about 1/3 of the proposed rule's benefits. Given the apparent rarity of such an incident, it is uncertain whether 20 years, 40 years, or some other time period is an appropriate assumption of the frequency of such an event. However, PHMSA did not account for this uncertainty in a sensitivity analysis.

Conclusions

Wetline incidents have ranged from minor incidents to serious accidents that have claimed lives and damaged property. Because PHMSA does not specifically provide an option to indicate a wetline incident on its incident reporting form, it is difficult to identify the number of wetline incidents from PHMSA's incident data. Additionally, due to inaccuracies in the data, the magnitude of the risk they pose to safety is also unclear. Although PHMSA has made changes to improve the quality of its incident data, the concerns we identified call into question the data's usefulness for characterizing key aspects of the benefits of avoiding these incidents, particularly the extent to which a wetlines rule would prevent fatalities. Furthermore, PHMSA's economic analysis does not account for these limitations. Thus, the analysis does not adequately convey the uncertainty of PHMSA's calculated benefit of the rule. Furthermore, PHMSA's analysis has not adequately addressed the market uncertainty with regard to the cost of the purging system, given that it is in limited use and the particular version of the system assumed in the analysis, to date, has not been in use.

While NTSB has called on PHMSA to address wetline risks, industry stakeholders have raised concerns about PHMSA's proposed regulation, particularly given that they view wetline incidents as occurring infrequently and that there could be other safety risks with the assumed option to address wetline safety risks. Without adjusting its cost-benefit analysis to account for the uncertainties due to the limited market for the purging system and limitations with PHMSA's incident data, the consequences of wetline incidents remain unclear and the costs and benefits of wetline regulation may not be accurately calculated in PHMSA's regulatory analysis.

Recommendations for Executive Action

To improve the reliability of data used to identify wetline incidents, we recommend that the Secretary of Transportation direct the Administrator of PHMSA to take the following two actions:

- Revise incident reporting to better capture wetline incidents and their consequences, such as by requiring specific reporting of wetline incidents by modifying the reporting form to include a specific indicator of such incidents, and adjusting the incident reporting form to indicate whether there are minimal costs versus no costs when costs are below the $500 reporting threshold.

- Address limitations with the accuracy and completeness of information used to assess the impact of wetline incidents, such as by specifying circumstances when PHMSA should seek missing cause and cost information, and potentially using sources other than the carrier to acquire information (such as investigations by local law enforcement or other federal agencies), particularly for the most severe incidents for which having accurate incident information is critical to oversight.

To strengthen the agency's rulemaking analysis, we recommend that the Secretary of Transportation direct the Administrator of PHMSA to take the following action:

- Strengthen the regulatory assessment of the proposed wetline rule's costs and benefits to better address the uncertainty of underlying factors. Such action could include incorporating more real-world information about purging systems or, if considered, other wetline solutions, and conducting additional sensitivity analyses for areas of uncertainty that are not addressed by improved data collection.

Agency Comments

We provided a draft of this report to the Department of Transportation for review and comment. DOT indicated that PHMSA would take this report into consideration as it continues to consider rulemaking and works to improve its incident data collection and internal review procedures. The department did not agree or disagree with our recommendations, but provided technical comments that we incorporated as appropriate.

We are sending copies of this report to the appropriate congressional committees, the Secretary of Transportation, and other interested parties. In addition, the report is available at no charge on the GAO website at http://www.gao.gov.

If you or your staff have any questions about this report, please contact me at (202) 512-2834 or flemings@gao.gov. Contact points for our Offices of Congressional Relations and Public Affairs may be found on the last page of this report. GAO staff who made key contributions to this report are listed in appendix III.

Susan A. Fleming
Director, Physical Infrastructure Issues

Appendix I: Objectives, Scope, and Methodology

Objectives	This report discusses (1) the extent that the Pipeline and Hazardous Materials Safety Administration's (PHMSA) data can be used to reliably identify wetline safety risks, (2) options for addressing wetline safety risks, and (3) how well PHMSA has assessed the costs and benefits of addressing these risks through regulation.
Scope and Methodology	To evaluate the extent that PHMSA's data reliably capture wetline incidents, we examined PHMSA's process for identifying wetline incidents and the data for the incidents that the agency has identified as being wetline-related occurring from the beginning of January 1999 to the end of March 2011. Our evaluation assessed PHMSA's efforts against federal internal control standards that require agencies to have relevant, reliable, and timely information for decision-making and external reporting purposes, and Office of Management and Budget (OMB) data quality guidelines for regulatory purposes.[1] Specifically, we analyzed the narrative information for these incidents to determine how useful this information is for identifying the incidents as being wetline-related. We examined the extent to which the incidents' coding of the component of the tank truck that failed could be indicative of a wetline incident. We also examined the extent to which these data accurately reported information about incident fatalities and to what extent they reported information about other incident damages. We selected 12 incidents to review as case studies to learn more about PHMSA's process for recording information about these incidents and to look for potential irregularities between PHMSA's database and other available information about the incidents. We selected these incidents to span the 1999 to 2011 time frame, to represent a range of minor to major incidents as measured by reported fatalities and other damages, and to include any incidents that were investigated by PHMSA or the National Transportation Safety Board (NTSB). We also included two incidents that PHMSA had determined to be wetline-related in its 2011 analysis but later determined not to be wetline incidents in its draft 2012 analysis.[2] We reviewed the reliability of

---

[1]GAO, *Standards for Internal Control in the Federal Government*, GAO/AIMD-00-21.3.1 (Washington, D.C.: November 1999); and Office of Management and Budget, *Regulatory Analysis,* OMB Circular No. A-4 (Sept. 17, 2003).

[2]For its January 2011 cost-benefit analysis, PHMSA identified wetline incidents occurring between January 1999 and December 2008. For its updated draft March 2012 assessment, PHMSA expanded its analysis to incidents occurring as of March 2011 and, in doing so, added some incidents to its list of wetline incidents but also removed some incidents in response to comments from stakeholders that questioned whether some of the incidents from the 2011 analysis were actually wetline incidents.

these incident data by examining them for missing data and inconsistencies, reviewing PHMSA's process for obtaining wetline data and maintaining them in the agency's database, and related internal controls. We concluded that the data were sufficiently reliable for the purposes of our report. Our conclusion that PHMSA's incident data are not sufficiently reliable for use in its regulatory analysis is independent of our conclusion that the data are sufficiently reliable for our purpose, since our purpose was to assess to what extent the data reliably identify wetline incidents and their characteristics. Based on the information PHMSA provided about how it uses these data for this purpose and the availability of PHMSA's incident data through its online incident database, we were able to make this assessment. We reviewed documents on and interviewed PHMSA officials about the agency's prior and ongoing efforts to improve the quality of its hazmat incident data.[3] Since our review focuses specifically on the issue of wetlines, we did not assess PHMSA's progress in improving its hazardous materials incident data in general.

To describe options to address wetline safety risks, we reviewed documentation from PHMSA's current and most recent prior related rulemaking efforts to identify what options have been proposed to address wetline safety risks and which major safety and industry stakeholders have been engaged on this issue. For contextual information about the feasibility of these options, we also visited a fuel terminal where cargo tank trucks are loaded. We reviewed documents from and interviewed associations and experts representing safety advocacy and various components of industry involved in the transportation of flammable liquids to understand stakeholder views on the options to address wetline safety risks. Specific stakeholders we interviewed are listed in table 4.

---

[3]During the course of our review, PHMSA officials told us they were involved in ongoing efforts to improve their incident data pursuant to deficiencies the agency had previously identified and hazardous material transportation incident data requirements in MAP-21. Consequently, we were not able to fully assess how these improvement efforts might affect their wetline incident data.

Table 4: Wetline Industry and Safety Stakeholders Interviewed

Industry stakeholder (segment)	Safety stakeholder (segment)[a]
• American Petroleum Institute (oil and natural gas industry)	• Advocates for Highway and Auto Safety (consumer, health, safety, and insurance alliance)
• American Trucking Associations (trucking industry)	• Bob Chipkevich (transportation safety consultant)
• Baltimore Cargo Tank Services (tank truck repair and service company)	• Commercial Vehicle Safety Alliance (association of government motor carrier safety officials)
• Dangerous Goods Advisory Council (hazardous materials transportation safety organization)	• International Association of Fire Chiefs (emergency response officials)
• Independent Fuel Terminal Operators Association (terminals for distributing flammable liquid products)	• International Brotherhood of Teamsters (labor union)
• International Liquid Terminals Association (terminals for distributing flammable and other liquid products)	• Joe Connelly (hazardous materials safety consultant)
• National Tank Truck Carriers (tank truck carriers)	• National Association of State Fire Marshals (state fire response officials)
• Petroleum Marketers Association of American (petroleum marketing trade associations)	• National Board of Boiler and Pressure Vessel Inspectors[b] (tank inspection, safety, training and standards)
• Renewable Fuels Association (ethanol producers)	• NTSB (federal incident investigation)[c]
• Society of Independent Gasoline Marketers of America (marketers of petroleum products)	• Truck Safety Coalition (public safety)
• Sunoco (petroleum marketer, carrier, and terminal operator)	
• Truck Trailer Manufacturers Association (tank truck manufacturers)	

Source: GAO.

[a]We contacted four other safety organizations that declined to be interviewed because they were not actively working on or did not have a position on the issue of wetline safety. These were American Association of Motor Vehicle Administrators, American Association of State Highway and Transportation Officials, Governors Highway Safety Association, and Insurance Institute for Highway Safety.

[b]We requested an interview with the National Board of Boiler and Pressure Vessel Inspectors, which instead provided written answers to our questions.

[c]Although NTSB is a government agency, in the context of this engagement we considered it a safety stakeholder due to its expertise having investigated wetline incidents and its recommendation that DOT prohibit wetlines.

We placed particular focus on examining the wetline purging system, since it is the option used in PHMSA's wetlines rulemaking analysis and the only option we are aware of that has been installed to address wetline risks. To better describe this option, we reviewed documentation about the system and interviewed the system manufacturer, Cargo Tank Concepts. We also interviewed stakeholders with direct experience with the system. We interviewed Sunoco—a petroleum marketer, carrier, and terminal operator that has installed the system on its tank truck fleet—and visited a Sunoco terminal near Philadelphia, Pennsylvania, that distributes flammable liquid products to tank trucks equipped with the purging system. We also interviewed Baltimore Cargo Tank Services, a tank service company that has installed the system on tank trucks. Based on reviews of patent applications and an industry trade publication, we identified other companies that may be able to produce similar wetline purging technology and interviewed two of them: Civacon and Franklin Fueling Systems.

Because most of the options to address wetline safety risks are theoretical—and the one solution that has been implemented is not widespread—our ability to present specific information about solutions' costs and benefits was limited. Instead, we focused on identifying to what extent stakeholders agree or disagree on information about these options, including the feasibility of implementing them in the current operating environment.

To evaluate how well PHMSA has assessed the costs and benefits of addressing wetline risks through regulation, we reviewed prior Department of Transportation rulemakings on wetlines to understand the history of the agency's work on this issue and focused our analysis on the current proposed rule, beginning with the Notice of Proposed Rulemaking that PHMSA issued in January 2011. We analyzed PHMSA's January 2011 cost-benefit analysis and an updated working draft version of the analysis from March 2012. We reviewed PHMSA's process and assumptions used for developing these analyses and the reasons for changes between them. We reviewed comments in the rulemaking record and interviewed stakeholders about their views on PHMSA's efforts to address wetline safety risks. We assessed PHMSA's efforts against OMB guidance for use of data and cost-benefit analysis to support rulemaking.[4]

---

[4]Office of Management and Budget, *Guidelines and Discount Rates for Benefit Cost Analysis of Federal Programs*, OMB Circular A-94, (revised 1992), and *Regulatory Analysis,* OMB Circular A-4, (Sept. 17, 2003).

We also reviewed PHMSA's non-regulatory efforts to address wetline
safety risks, which consisted of an effort to raise awareness of emergency
responders, following the agency's withdrawal of its most recent prior
proposed rule in 2006.

We conducted this performance audit from September 2012 to
September 2013 in accordance with generally accepted government
auditing standards. Those standards require that we plan and perform the
audit to obtain sufficient, appropriate evidence to provide a reasonable
basis for our findings and conclusions based on our audit objectives. We
believe that the evidence obtained provides a reasonable basis for our
findings and conclusions based on our audit objectives.

Appendix II: PHMSA's Wetline Proposed-Rule Cost-Benefit Methodology and Related Changes

To support its proposed wetline rule, PHMSA developed analyses of the rule's costs and benefits: PHMSA released a first analysis with the proposed rule in January 2011 and provided us a working draft of an updated analysis from March 2012 that the agency did not release publicly. In updating its cost-benefit analysis in 2012, PHMSA made several changes to its methodology for calculating costs and benefits that affect the outcomes of the analysis and may affect the ability to compare its scenarios.

Both the 2011 and 2012 analyses are built on the assumption that tank trucks have a useful life of 20 years. Therefore, the entire tank truck fleet in existence at the time of a rule's effective date would presumably be replaced during the course of the 20 years that followed. The 2011 and draft 2012 analyses include four alternative scenarios with varying time periods for achieving compliance with the proposed rule—specifically in 5, 10, 15, or 20 years. Were a rule to require compliance within 20 years, carriers could achieve compliance by equipping only new trucks with a wetline purging system. If compliance were required sooner, some degree of retrofitting of existing tank trucks would be required, in addition to equipping any vehicles that are new in the compliance timeframe.

All four scenarios in the 2011 analysis were analyzed over a 20-year timeframe. The primary cost in the 2011 analysis is the installation of wetline purging systems over a 20-year period, which included all new tank trucks during that time and, in the case of the three shorter compliance scenarios, the additional cost of retrofitting some tank trucks that would not have been replaced by the time compliance was required. Benefits in the 2011 analysis were the value of associated fatalities and other damages from wetline incidents the rule is assumed to avoid over the 20-year period. In the 2011 analysis, benefits are greater in the shorter compliance scenarios because tank trucks are equipped with purging systems sooner and therefore more incidents are avoided. In the 20-year scenario, only 5 percent of trucks are equipped each year so it takes until year 20 when all vehicles would be equipped and all incidents in that year would be avoided.[1] In contrast, in the 5-year compliance scenario, by year 5, all future incidents are assumed to be avoided, resulting in greater estimated benefit, but also increased cost, due to the

---

[1]In the 20-year compliance scenario, since it assumed tank trucks have a useful life of 20 years, only new tank trucks are equipped with the wetline purging system, resulting in an equal number of new trucks being equipped with the system and all trucks equipped by the end of the 20 years.

need to equip sooner—requiring many trucks to be retrofit with purging systems—and the continued cost of equipping trucks in years 6-20 as retrofitted trucks need replacement.

In contrast, the 2012 cost-benefit analysis did not calculate all costs and benefits of the rule over a 20-year period, but rather calculated costs for each truck required to be equipped with a purging system within the compliance time frame and the benefits associated with that equipage for the remaining life of each equipped truck. This changes the number of years over which costs and benefits are calculated:

- For the 20-year compliance scenario, the 2012 analysis includes costs for equipping all new tank trucks purchased during the 20 years, and measures benefits for 20 years after each truck is equipped. That is, a truck that is bought new in year 15 will have benefits associated with that equipage until year 35.

- For the 5-year compliance scenario, all trucks are either equipped new or retrofit during the first 5 years, and the benefits associated with the remaining life of that truck are assessed. While trucks purchased new in those 5 years will have benefits measured over the 20-year life of each truck, the benefits associated with the retrofit trucks are calculated for a shorter period of time depending on PHMSA's assumptions about the remaining life of those vehicles. Benefits accrue until a retrofitted truck is presumed retired from service.

PHMSA did not include in its 2012 assessment the costs or benefits associated with a new truck that would replace the truck that had been retrofit. For example, if a truck was retrofit in year 3 of the analysis and it was assumed that it had a remaining life of 10 years, benefits associated with that truck were included in the analysis only through year 13; the costs from equipping a new replacement truck in year 13 and the resulting benefits thereafter were not included. Consequently, the 2012 analysis may not be comparable with the 2011 analysis, which used the same 20-year time-frame for the four scenarios.[2] Further, this methodology does not show that equipping trucks sooner would result in greater societal benefit, likely because benefits are not included for new

---

[2]In cost-benefit analyses, projects (or in this case, different compliance-date scenarios) should always be compared over the same discounting period since projects with different time frames are not directly comparable. Anthony E. Boardman et al., *Cost-Benefit Analysis*, 2nd Ed. (Upper Saddle River, N.J.: Prentice Hall, 2001), p. 133.

trucks that would replace retrofit trucks retired within the 20 year timeframe. Rather, it shows the value of benefits as greater under the longer compliance timeframe. In contrast, the 2011 analysis shows greater benefit for the 5-year compliance scenario than the 20-year scenario, but at significantly higher cost. Table 5 compares the cost and benefit values and calculation methods for the 20-year and 5-year compliance scenarios in PHMSA's 2011 and 2012 analyses.

Table 5: Cost and Benefit Values and Calculation Methodologies from PHMSA's 2011 and 2012 Wetline Proposed-Rule Cost-Benefit Analyses

	2011 analysis		2012 analysis	
	20-year compliance scenario	5-year compliance scenario	20-year compliance scenario	5-year compliance scenario
Costs[a]	$52.5 million. Cost based on equipping only new trucks, resulting in 27,000 equipages that occur over 20 years.	$100.6 million. Cost based on equipping new trucks, resulting in 27,000 new equipages that occur over 20 years, and retrofitting existing trucks in use by the end of the first 5 years, resulting in 20,500 retrofits over the first 5 years.	$65.4 million. Cost is based on equipping only new trucks, resulting in 27,000 equipages that occur over 20 years.	$74.6 million. Cost is based on equipping new trucks during the first 5 years and retrofitting all other trucks during that period, resulting in 27,000 equipages over 5 years.
Benefits[a]	$51.6 million. Benefits are the value of wetline incidents avoided during the 20-year period. Thus, with an equal number of new trucks equipped each year, more incidents are avoided in later years than in early years.	$94.7 million. Benefits are the value of wetline incidents avoided during the 20-year period. Thus, all wetline incidents are avoided after the first 5 years, since all trucks are equipped by the fifth year, and a percentage of incidents are avoided each of the first 5 years based on how many trucks would be equipped that year.	$67.3 million. Benefits are calculated for the useful life of each equipage: thus benefits are calculated for 20 years for every truck, since all equipages are on new trucks expected to last 20 years.	$54.1 million. Benefits are calculated for the useful life of each equipage: thus benefits are calculated for 20 years for every new truck, and for fewer years for each retrofitted truck.

Source: GAO analysis of PHMSA cost-benefit analyses

[a]Values are present value 2009 dollars PHMSA discounted using a 3 percent discount rate. PHMSA also calculated costs and benefits using a 7 percent discount rate.

Appendix III: GAO Contact and Staff Acknowledgments

GAO Contact	Susan A. Fleming, 202-512-2834, flemings@gao.gov
Staff Acknowledgments	In addition to the individual named above, Sara Vermillion, Assistant Director; Amy Abramowitz; Melissa Bodeau; Geoff Hamilton; Andrew Huddleston; Tara Jayant; SaraAnn Moessbauer; Jaclyn Nelson; Josh Ormond; Madhav Panwar; Lisa Shibata; and Anne Stevens made key contributions to this report.

GAO's Mission	The Government Accountability Office, the audit, evaluation, and investigative arm of Congress, exists to support Congress in meeting its constitutional responsibilities and to help improve the performance and accountability of the federal government for the American people. GAO examines the use of public funds; evaluates federal programs and policies; and provides analyses, recommendations, and other assistance to help Congress make informed oversight, policy, and funding decisions. GAO's commitment to good government is reflected in its core values of accountability, integrity, and reliability.
Obtaining Copies of GAO Reports and Testimony	The fastest and easiest way to obtain copies of GAO documents at no cost is through GAO's website (http://www.gao.gov). Each weekday afternoon, GAO posts on its website newly released reports, testimony, and correspondence. To have GAO e-mail you a list of newly posted products, go to http://www.gao.gov and select "E-mail Updates."
Order by Phone	The price of each GAO publication reflects GAO's actual cost of production and distribution and depends on the number of pages in the publication and whether the publication is printed in color or black and white. Pricing and ordering information is posted on GAO's website, http://www.gao.gov/ordering.htm. Place orders by calling (202) 512-6000, toll free (866) 801-7077, or TDD (202) 512-2537. Orders may be paid for using American Express, Discover Card, MasterCard, Visa, check, or money order. Call for additional information.
Connect with GAO	Connect with GAO on Facebook, Flickr, Twitter, and YouTube. Subscribe to our RSS Feeds or E-mail Updates. Listen to our Podcasts. Visit GAO on the web at www.gao.gov.
To Report Fraud, Waste, and Abuse in Federal Programs	Contact: Website: http://www.gao.gov/fraudnet/fraudnet.htm E-mail: fraudnet@gao.gov Automated answering system: (800) 424-5454 or (202) 512-7470
Congressional Relations	Katherine Siggerud, Managing Director, siggerudk@gao.gov, (202) 512-4400, U.S. Government Accountability Office, 441 G Street NW, Room 7125, Washington, DC 20548
Public Affairs	Chuck Young, Managing Director, youngc1@gao.gov, (202) 512-4800 U.S. Government Accountability Office, 441 G Street NW, Room 7149 Washington, DC 20548

Please Print on Recycled Paper.